CRIME AND SOCIAL JUSTICE
IN INDIAN COUNTRY

Indigenous Justice

MARIANNE O. NIELSEN AND KAREN JARRATT-SNIDER
Series Editors

EDITED BY
MARIANNE O. NIELSEN AND
KAREN JARRATT-SNIDER

CRIME AND
SOCIAL JUSTICE IN
INDIAN COUNTRY

THE UNIVERSITY OF
ARIZONA PRESS

TUCSON

The University of Arizona Press
www.uapress.arizona.edu

© 2018 by The Arizona Board of Regents
All rights reserved. Published 2018

ISBN-13: 978-0-8165-3781-5 (paper)

Cover design by Leigh McDonald
Cover art: *Chavatangakwuna / Short Rainbow* by Lomayumtewa K. Ishii

Library of Congress Cataloging-in-Publication Data are available at the Library of Congress.

Printed in the United States of America
♾ This paper meets the requirements of ANSI/NISO Z39.48-1992 (Permanence of Paper).

This book is dedicated to our patient partners, Larry Gould and Gary Snider, and to the Native American scholars who are doing such necessary and innovative research for Native American communities.

CONTENTS

ACKNOWLEDGMENTS

WE WOULD LIKE to express our gratitude to the authors who contributed to this book. It took a while to get it into print, and we appreciate your willingness to stick with the project and continue to trust that we would get your work out there. We would like to acknowledge Northern Arizona University for its commitment to Native American students and communities, and for encouraging projects such as this. We would also like to express our gratitude to Sara Lee for her invaluable help. As well, we want to say thank you to three anonymous reviewers who gave us some excellent advice, and to the good people at University of Arizona Press who believed in this project to the point of being willing to publish another two (and maybe more) books in the series.

CRIME AND SOCIAL JUSTICE IN INDIAN COUNTRY

INTRODUCTION

MARIANNE O. NIELSEN AND
KAREN JARRATT-SNIDER

NDIGENOUS PEOPLES in the United States are nearly invisible in discussions of criminal and social justice. The focus is usually on African Americans or Hispanic Americans, mainly because their numbers are much larger within the general population and within the criminal justice system. Whether the discussion is about offenders, victims, or service providers, American Indians are usually left out. Their numbers are lumped into the "Other" category in government statistics, unless they are the subjects of a special report that may come out once every ten years or so (see, for example, Perry 2004). Otherwise, the issues of criminal justice that touch their lives and communities are ignored except by a handful of scholars and the community members themselves. In other colonized countries such as Canada, Australia, and New Zealand, this is not the case. There, Indigenous peoples are *the* population of concern for the government in the criminal justice and social justice arenas, and the proliferation of studies and reports reflect that. This book provides one small restorative dose for the neglect of American Indian criminal and social justice issues in the United States.

Criminal and social justice are essential areas of study as they relate to Native Americans or American Indians or Indigenous peoples, terms we use interchangeably.[1] Indigenous Americans are a population with a unique political and legal status, whose justice issues—and solutions—are rooted in colonialism. The long and terrible process of colonization destroyed not only the lives and communities of Indigenous peoples in the United States and around the globe but also their human, legal, and civil rights. As examples of important American justice issues, more than any other group, Native American women are proportionately more likely to be sexually assaulted by white men, Native Americans are more likely to be arrested for alcohol-related offenses than any other offenses, and Native American communities suffer more than any other communities from environmental crimes such as the dumping of toxic materials like uranium tailings and lead chat.[2] These issues have their roots in injustices first perpetrated during colonization.

Indigenous peoples, to borrow from Canadian lawyer Bradford W. Morse (1989, 1), are "all people who trace their ancestors in these lands to time immemorial." This includes individuals of part-Indigenous ancestry and individuals who live away from ancestral lands. In the United States, these Indigenous peoples are referred to as Native Americans (which includes Native Hawaiians, Inuit, and Alaska Natives), as American Indians, or, most respectfully, by the name of their nation. In Canada they are Aboriginal peoples, First Nations, Métis, or again, the people of their nation. In New Zealand, they are Māori; in Australia, they are Indigenous Australians. There are Indigenous peoples in any country that has been colonized—Brazil, China, Greenland, Mexico, Mongolia, Norway, South Africa, Taiwan, Zambia, and a very long list that could follow. They share many characteristics; many members of their populations are marginalized, that is, lacking economic, social, and political power; are impoverished due to exploitation and loss of resources; are stereotyped and suffer from discrimination; have a history of coerced assimilation by the colonizing state; have little autonomy and self-determination; are recovering from serious social disorganization caused by the loss of population due to violence, the loss of culture due to coerced assimilation, and the loss of social institutions due to imposed laws; and are overrepresented in the criminal justice systems of their country as offenders and victims.[3] As a result of this history, criminal justice for Indigenous peoples is intricately interwoven with social justice. Social and criminal justice issues for Indigenous peoples are different from those of other disadvantaged populations because the history that caused them is different. The solutions to the issues must also be different if they are going to be effective.

This book mainly encompasses the research on issues of social and criminal justice in the United States, and the innovative responses of

Indigenous communities, although some chapters bring in comparisons to other countries. The historical contexts used are from Indigenous points of view. An important assumption of this book and its authors is that colonization was one long historical injustice and today's justice issues for Indigenous peoples are rooted in it. Intergenerational post-traumatic stress disorder, caused by colonial violence and powerlessness, for example, is likely one of the foundational causes of the internal and externalized violence committed by Indigenous individuals (Duran 2006). In other words, when previous generations of family and community have barely survived massacres, starvation, assimilation, rape, loss of culture, loss of identity, and loss of control over their own lives, the psychological, physical, and spiritual impacts persist for generations, leading to Indigenous individuals committing violence against themselves, for example, through alcohol abuse or suicide, or committing violence against others, such as child neglect and domestic violence. Such factors still have an impact today so that, in 2012, more Native Americans (29 percent) lived in poverty than did the U.S. population (16 percent) overall (U.S. Census Bureau 2013). About 21 percent of Native Americans and Alaska Natives twenty-five and older do not have a high school education, compared with 14 percent of the total population (U.S. Census Bureau 2013). The Native unemployment rate is almost double the national rate (11 percent compared to 6.2 percent) (Peralta 2014). Bachman (1992) found that high rates of suicide, family violence, and alcohol abuse are also characteristic of some Native communities. Suicide, for example, is three times higher than the national average, and up to ten times higher on some reservations (Horowitz 2014). These are criminogenic living conditions: that is, they put member of these communities at higher risk of getting involved with the criminal justice system.[4]

In more general terms, Native communities are among the most marginalized, economically, politically, and socially, in the United States. To add insult to injury, they are constrained by more laws than any other diverse group. Many human rights and justice-related issues are unique to Indigenous America because of the special legal status of Native Americans and the highly complex jurisdictional issues resulting from colonial ideologies being institutionalized into federal law and policy. For example, contradictory shifts in federal Indian policy from 1830 to 1934 resulted in several land statuses being present within a single tribal jurisdictional area, which today lead to complex problems in finding resolutions to environmental and criminal justice issues and for tribal nations trying to exercise sovereignty around economic development opportunities.

This example brings to the forefront another justice issue for Indigenous people—treatment by the criminal justice system. Due to the various shifts in U.S. federal Indian policy from the 1850s to the 1970s and various changes in federal laws, criminal jurisdiction in Indian Country—in the legal sense of the term—means that many Native Americans fall subject to state laws and prosecution, rather than that of their own Indigenous nation, even when a crime falls within the borders of their tribe. Issues of institutional and individual discrimination range from discriminatory laws, to the indifference of criminal justice personnel to homeless Indigenous individuals (see, for example, Razack 2015), to stereotyping, to brutality. Injustices also occur in arrest, sentencing, and incarceration, although the research is lacking and what exists is contradictory (Nielsen and Robyn 2018).

After all these justice issues are recounted, it is not surprising that male American Indian prisoners comprise about 16 percent of all federal prisoners even though Native Americans make up only 2 percent of the total U.S. population (Perry 2004; U.S. Census Bureau 2012). Although statistics are hard to find, indications are that Native American women and juveniles are also overrepresented in prisons (Ross 1998; Martin 2014). Overrepresentation in the criminal justice system is an unfortunate fact that has been acknowledged for quite some time, but Indigenous justice issues have not been as thoroughly researched as those of the other diverse groups mentioned earlier.

It is important to focus on the resilience Indigenous people and peoples have shown in dealing with these issues. Community and individual resilience occurs as communities use their culture and values to develop innovative programs that communicate pride in their culture and history to young people and adults and thereby perhaps keep them from reoffending. Individual resilience is seen, for example, in the growing educational achievement rates (U.S. Census Bureau 2013) and dropping crime rates in Indian Country (Silverman 2009).

The lack of current-day criminal justice research may be partly due to the few scholars familiar with the culturally appropriate research protocols developed by Indigenous communities and institutions; however, the growing wave of young Native American scholars and some non-Indigenous scholars understand and use these in their research. This means they have access where many other scholars do not because they abide by the sovereign rights of Native nations and develop their research projects accordingly. The editors are delighted to provide these scholars with an opportunity to gather their work in this book and share their knowledge not only with students, professionals, and other scholars but with Indigenous community members throughout the United States and globally. There are too few Indigenous voices represented in the criminal justice literature, which affects both the visibility of Indigenous scholarship and its practitioners. Indigenous voices and stories are important to add to the discussion because their research interests are often based on their very real experiences with the issues.

Indigenous justice as it is presented in this book (and the books to follow in the series) is a concept with many facets. It deals with the past, present, and future. It includes crimes by and against individuals. It investigates crimes by organizations and governments against communities. It analyzes laws, both Indigenous and colonial-settler. It focuses on ways of achieving justice, both traditional and European based. It examines the taking away of rights and the reassertion of rights, including health, safety, law, economic development, and community and individual resilience. It describes new and innovative approaches to achieving justice so that some of the most talked-about and imitated justice, environmental, and social service programs in non-Indigenous justice systems have their roots in Indigenous community processes and principles such as peacemaking, juvenile sentencing circles, healing lodges (minimum security prisons), and environmental responsibility to future generations.

The responses to Indigenous justice issues encompass both social control and healing, but most of all, they deal with healing and all that healing encompasses, including restoration of lives and communities, reassertion of rights, self-determination, and sovereignty. To Indigenous people and peoples, these are everyday, almost simple concepts, but sometimes it is necessary to remind people of their existence. In spring 2016, the co-editors attended a talk by Dr. Raymond Austin at the Native American Cultural Center at Northern Arizona University. Dr. Austin spoke about the concept of sovereignty as seen by the Navajo Nation. At the end of his talk he asked a simple yet profound question (that we are paraphrasing): "What does sovereignty mean to Indigenous peoples?" It is a simple question with a seemingly simple answer, but it is a question that has not been asked by non-Indigenous lawmakers. It is a question that Indigenous scholars and decision makers wrestle with because of the long assimilation process to which they and their ancestors have been subjected. And of course, there are as many perspectives on sovereignty, and crime and social justice, as there are Indigenous nations, cultures, and individuals.

In looking at responses to Indigenous justice issues, it is important to remember that Indigenous peoples remain in danger of losing their sovereignty; their right to rebuild their nations; their right to govern themselves on their own lands; and their right to determine their own lives, development, identities, and responses to issues. Sovereignty is therefore one of the important themes of this book relating to issues of social and criminal justice.

THEMES OF THE BOOK

As mentioned, **sovereignty**, or the right to make decisions about one's own citizens, is one of the most important themes found in every chapter in one form or another. Additionally, self-determination, the right to make decisions about one's own culture and life, and how to respond to issues, is also a prominent theme throughout the book. Both can be negotiated and practiced through many channels, including sports (Ali-Joseph), tribal codes (Luna-Gordinier), state law (Hiraldo), and juvenile justice (Luna-Firebaugh and Luna-Gordinier). Non-Indigenous governments need to develop meaningful relationships with Indigenous governing bodies, especially when they provide justice services to overlapping populations.

Criminal jurisdiction is an important aspect of sovereignty. The current jurisdictional maze among federal, state, and tribal justice authorities that afflicts Indian Country leads to many social and criminal issues (for example, the need for stalking legislation, as discussed by Luna-Gordinier). Nations need the legal freedom to use their culture in justice decision making and to develop innovative healing programs rooted in Indigenous cultures, such as the juvenile justice programs described by

Luna-Firebaugh and Luna-Gordinier. As Smith (cited by Bennett) states, part of sovereignty is the ability to act sovereign.

American Indian individuals, communities, and organizations in the past and continuing today have a great deal of **resilience**. Ali-Joseph in her chapter on sports as a practice of everyday sovereignty emphasizes that Indigenous resilience has led to the endurance and adaptation of American Indian peoples to colonial assimilative practices that led to social injustice. She points to the important role that sports play in providing American Indian young people with pride in their identity and an access to education as it opens the doors to learning new skills and coping with discrimination.

Pride in an **Indigenous identity** is related to resilience. Ali-Joseph discusses how pride in identity is negotiated in sports. According to Bennett, a solid Indigenous identity is important in responding to modern-day stereotypes related to crime such as those that afflict the so-called casino tribes. Luna-Firebaugh and Luna-Gordinier describe the importance of pride in Indigenous identity and culture for preventing Indigenous youth recidivism in Arizona and New Zealand. Archambeault describes how Indigenous identity has been attacked through colonial processes and how naming has worked to divide the interests of Indigenous peoples.

Resistance to the social injustice caused by the assimilation and disempowerment that have been overt and covert agendas of colonial governments is found in many arenas. It is one aspect of exercising sovereignty and maintaining Indigenous identity. Several of the authors give examples of how this resistance occurs; Hiraldo uses the example of the political negotiations over the Indian Child Welfare Act in North Carolina to show how American Indians have resisted assimilation by creating their own political space. Ali-Joseph discusses how sports were used to resist assimilation in boarding schools for American Indian children.

The sometimes different experiences by **gender** of the social injustice that results from colonialism is another theme. Women athletes, for example, must not only deal with discrimination against American Indians, but against women, according to Ali-Joseph. As Robyn describes, the social harm resulting from the involuntary sterilization of Native women affected both them as individuals and Native peoples as a population, and as Bennett describes, Native women are disproportionately the victims of violence in border towns.

Several underlying themes become apparent when the works within the book are treated as a whole. The **involvement of the community** in initiatives to counteract crime and social injustice is clearly exemplified by Luna-Firebaugh and Luna-Gordinier's chapter on effective juvenile programs. It underlies the importance of sports for Indigenous communities in Ali-Joseph's chapter. It also underlies discussions of, for example, gaming development (Bennett), the resolution of legal issues (Hiraldo), and the fight against hate crimes in border towns (Bennett).

The need to **overcome social injustice resulting from marginalization** is another underlying theme. This marginalization may be legal, as in Hiraldo's, Luna-Gordinier's, and Luna-Firebaugh and Luna-Gordinier's chapters; economic, as in Bennett's chapter on gaming; political, as in Archambeault's chapter; and social, as in chapters by Robyn on sterilization and Bennett on hate crimes. Indigenous communities and individuals were deliberately marginalized by settler-colonists to gain access to Indigenous lands and resources, that is, to steal them since most of them were obtained through fraudulent and violent means. They are now mostly unrecoverable, but many aspects of Indigenous life are resilient and are not gone, in fact are being revitalized, such as political power; new economic development opportunities; and cultural teachings, languages, and identities—all of which have positive impacts on the handling of crime and social injustice. Nations are being rebuilt on Indigenous land, and for the 70-plus percent of Indigenous individuals who do not live on ancestral lands, there are new ways to participate through the media, urban justice programs and organizations, and educational institutions.

The importance of having **Indigenous perspectives** in all areas of social and criminal justice research is another underlying theme. Indigenous researchers ask questions that are unthinkable (literally) by non-Indigenous scholars. Much like Dr. Ray Austin's question about what sovereignty means to Indigenous peoples, some questions are unthinkable by researchers educated from a colonial perspective. A reoccurring issue in criminal justice especially is the imposition of solutions from the top down, and with few exceptions, the top is populated by descendants of white northern European colonizers immersed in a worldview that proclaims the colonial way of thinking to be the correct one. Perhaps that is why so many justice initiatives in Indian Country have failed—Indigenous peoples have not been included, consulted, or allowed control of justice initiatives, at least not in any meaningful way. Another reason is that Indigenous researchers focus on issues that may be ignored or given little value by most non-Indigenous researchers. In some ways, they represent the priorities of Indigenous communities. An example is the previously "unthinkable" questions about border town hate crimes against women that Bennett asks or the sterilization of Native women that Robyn describes. Indigenous researchers also ask remarkable questions about discriminatory laws, lack of health and treatment services for social problems, and the role of cultural identity and healing in crime prevention and rehabilitation programming.

Not only is it important to have the perspective of Indigenous researchers, it is perhaps even more important to have the **voices of Indigenous individuals, organizations, and communities** through excerpts from interviews, documents from Indigenous organizations and websites, and autobiographical writings. Many of the researchers gathered at least part of their data from members of Indigenous communities.

Finally, an important theme is **global comparisons**. Indigenous peoples around the globe are finding common goals in dealing with crime and social justice issues. Communication is increasing exponentially, and strategies and solutions are being shared. One vital step is comparative research such as that carried out by Luna-Firebaugh and Luna-Gordinier, whose findings may prove invaluable for the examination of the same issues in other colonized countries.

THE BOOK

The chapters in this book represent important research in the field of Indigenous justice into issues that are ongoing. As one Native elder said to Nielsen, "Problems that took 400 years to develop can't be solved in the four-year term of a politician." The authors in this volume are beginning and longtime scholars, the majority of whom are Native American. The chapters reflect the wide array of research being done in locations across the United States and outside the country. In the broadest terms, the book reflects important Indigenous issues in three key areas: crime, social justice, and community responses to crime and justice issues.

This book is the first in a three-book series on Indigenous justice. The next book in the series will focus on issues in Indigenous law, including traditional, national, and international law, and the third book will focus on environmental issues.

NOTES

1. We use these terms interchangeably unless a specific population is the topic. It is important to note, however, that each of these terms has important political, legal, and social nuances, some of which can be extremely harmful to people, as explained by Archambeault in chapter 4.

2. For statistics on these issues, see Greenfield and Smith (1999) about sexual assault against American Indian women and Silverman (2009) about alcohol-related crimes. For information on Indigenous environmental issues, see the Environmental Protection Agency's website and their Office of Compliance and Enforcement website.

3. For excellent histories from an Indigenous point of view, see, for example, Walker (1990) for New Zealand, Mudrooroo (1995) for Australia, Monchalin (2016) for Canada, and Dunbar-Ortiz (2015) for the United States. A good overview of colonization globally is Coates's *A Global History of Indigenous Peoples* (2004). For information on the relationship between colonization and current Indigenous justice issues, see, for example, the Truth and Reconciliation Commission of Canada (2015) and the National Inquiry . . . (1997) for Australia.

4. See Ross (2014) for overviews of the marginalizations faced by many of today's American Indian population.

REFERENCES

Bachman, Ronet. 1992. *Death and Violence on the Reservation: Homicide, Family Violence and Suicide in American Indian Populations*. New York: Auburn.

Coates, Ken S. 2004. *A Global History of Indigenous Peoples*. New York: Palgrave Macmillan.

Dunbar-Ortiz, Roxanne. 2015. *An Indigenous Peoples' History of the United States*. Boston: Beacon Press.

Duran, Eduardo. 2006. *Healing the Soul Wound*. New York: Teachers College Press.

Greenfield, Lawrence A., and Steven K. Smith. 1999. *American Indians and Crime*. Washington, D.C.: Bureau of Justice Statistics, U.S. Department of Justice.

Horowitz, S. 2014. "The Hard Lives—and High Suicide Rate—of Native American Children on Reservations." *Washington Post*, March 9. https://www

.washingtonpost.com/world/national-security/the-hard-lives--and-high
-suicide-rate--of-native-american-children/2014/03/09/6e0ad9b2-9f03-11e3
-b8d8-94577ff66b28_story.html?utm_term=.523740ce3730.

Martin, Favian Alejandro. 2014. Native Youth Delinquency. In *American Indians at Risk*, ed. Jeffrey Ian Ross, 135–52. Santa Barbara, CA: Greenwood.

Monchalin, Lisa. 2016. *The Colonial Problem: An Indigenous Perspective on Crime and Injustice in Canada*. Toronto, ON: University of Toronto Press.

Morse, Bradford W., ed. 1989. *Aboriginal Peoples and the Law: Indian, Métis and Inuit Rights in Canada*, rev. 1st ed. Ottawa, ON: Carleton University Press.

Mudrooroo. 1995. *Us Mob: History, Culture, Struggle: An Introduction to Indigenous Australia*. Sydney, NSW: Angus and Robertson.

National Inquiry into the Separation of Aboriginal and Torres Strait Islander Children from Their Families. 1997. *Bringing Them Home*. Canberra, ACT: Commonwealth of Australia.

Nielsen, Marianne O., and Linda Robyn. 2018. Stolen Lands, Stolen Lives. In *Investigating Difference*, 3rd ed., ed. Sarah Prior and Lynn Jones, 175–89. New York: Pearson.

Peralta, Katherine. 2014. Native Americans Left Behind in the Economic Recovery. *U.S. News & World Report*. http://www.usnews.com/news/articles/2014/11/27/native-americans-left-behind-in-the-economic-recovery.

Perry, Steven W. 2004. *American Indians and Crime: A BJS Statistical Profile, 1992–2002*. NCJ 203097. Washington, D.C.: U.S. Department of Justice.

Razack, Sherene H. 2015. *Dying from Improvement: Inquests and Inquiries into Indigenous Deaths in Custody*. Toronto, ON: University of Toronto Press.

Ross, Jeffrey Ian, ed. 2014. *American Indians at Risk*. Santa Barbara, CA: Greenwood.

Ross, Luana. 1998. *Inventing the Savage*. Austin: University of Texas Press.

Silverman, Robert A. 2009. Patterns of Native American Crime 1984–2005. In *Criminal Justice in Native America*, ed. Marianne O. Nielsen and Robert A. Silverman, 18–31. Tucson: University of Arizona Press.

Truth and Reconciliation Commission of Canada. 2015. *Final Report of the Truth and Reconciliation Commission of Canada, Volume One: Summary*. Toronto, ON: James Lorimer.

U.S. Census Bureau. 2012. "The American Indian and Alaska Native Population: 2010." www.census.gov/prod/cen2010/briefs/c2010br-10.pdf.

U.S. Census Bureau. 2013. "Facts for Features: American Indian and Alaska Native Heritage Month, November 2013." www.census.gov/newsroom/facts-for-features/2014/cb13-ff26.html.

Walker, Ranguini. 1990. *Ka Whawhai Tonu Matou: Struggle Without End*. Auckland, NZ: Penguin.

PART I

CRIME

INTRODUCTION BY MARIANNE O. NIELSEN AND KAREN JARRATT-SNIDER

Crime is an important issue in Indian Country and in Indigenous communities globally. Because of colonial processes and the political, economic, and social marginalization that resulted, some Indigenous communities suffer from various criminogenic factors, that is, factors that contribute to criminal offending, such as poverty, drug and alcohol abuse, and post-traumatic stress. There is no way to predict whether a person will commit a criminal act, but it is possible to describe factors that place people at more risk and at less risk. Indigenous communities are working hard to develop programs to increase individual resilience, that is, put people at less risk.

Indigenous communities have been the victims of crime since colonization began in addition to having their human rights violated, for example, losing their lands through fraudulent treaties and outright theft, and losing their lives through murder and massacres. They were also subject to cultural genocide due to laws and policies forbidding the practice of their spiritual ceremonies, their form of leadership and economic structure, their social institutions including family structures, and the use of their language. This list applies a social harm perspective (defined shortly) on crime since these laws and policies were legal (though sometimes abused in such a way that they became crimes, such as sexual abuse in boarding schools), but legal or not, they did nearly irreparable damage to Indigenous culture and practices. The key word here, however, is *nearly*. Indigenous peoples have shown their resilience over the centuries in revitalizing their cultures, languages, and practices, and using them as the basis for justice programs, among other social institutions.

The kinds of crime that occur in Indigenous communities can be divided into two categories: those perpetrated by Indigenous people and those by non-Indigenous people. One definition of crime is legalistic in that it relies on law as defined by the non-Indigenous justice system: "A crime is held to be an offense which goes beyond the personal and into the public sphere, breaking prohibitory rules or laws, to which legitimate punishments or sanctions are attached, and which requires the intervention of a public authority (the state or a local body)" (Marshall 1994, 96). This definition, however, ignores the important consideration that those in power can use the law to define their harmful acts so that they are not criminal. The social harm perspective is particularly important in discussions of crimes against Indigenous people and peoples since it focuses on inequality in its definition of crime: "Crime must be defined in a way that evaluates wrongful behaviors on the basis of the *severity of the harm done* regardless of the class origin of the offense" (Michalowski 1985, 405, emphasis in the original). The social harm perspective defines crime as some acts that are legal since they cause great harm to the victims, for example, unsafe working conditions that lead to employee deaths or unsafe consumer products that lead to infants dying.

Bennett's chapter on hate crimes against Native American women in border towns provides a clear example of crimes against Indigenous people as defined legalistically, although the social harms to both individuals and communities are also evident. Violence against Native women in border towns is clearly a criminal act, and because of the motivating colonial ideology (now racism), it can also be seen as a hate crime in the common usage of that term. Simply put, Indigenous people are the victims of ethnoviolence such as hate crimes because of their Indigenous status. It should be noted that they are also the victims of microaggressions, that is, the "everyday verbal, nonverbal, and environmental slights, snubs, or insults, whether intentional or unintentional, that communicate hostile, derogatory, or negative messages to target persons based solely upon their marginalized group membership" (Sue 2010, 3). These acts have a cumulative effect than can contribute to post-traumatic stress, as well as ill health (Sue 2010). They are a social harm related to hate crime but not a crime.

Robyn's chapter on the involuntary sterilization of Indigenous women not only illustrates the close line between legalistic and social harm definitions of crime but also invokes violations of Indigenous human rights discussed further in the introduction to part II.

Bennett's chapter on gaming gives a solid example of the misconceptions and stereotypes regarding Indigenous sovereignty and crime, as well as illustrates the use of law to control Indian economic and other development. The competing interests of Indian nations, states, and non-Indian gaming enterprises have forced Indian nations to negotiate with state and federal governments in order to develop this form of economic enterprise. Class III gaming compacts have been called by some an infringement on the sovereign rights of American Indian nations and a form of state extortion in that the Indian Gaming Regulatory Act (IGRA) of 1988 requires Indian nations to sign over a percentage of their Class III gaming profits in exchange for state cooperation with their gaming enterprises. As Light and Rand (2005, 3) state, "From a tribal perspective . . . Indian gaming law and policy is the result of one-sided 'negotiations' that impose state and federal law on tribes in direct contravention of tribal authority." Nevertheless, gaming remains a viable and important economic activity for some Indian tribal nations.

One fact that often gets forgotten in discussions of community responses to crime and social justice issues is that 78 percent of Native Americans live away from American Indian land (U.S.

Census Bureau 2012, 12) and that federal laws only apply to individuals who are from federally recognized nations. The laws do not apply to people from state-recognized nations or the many unrecognized Native American/American Indian groups such as those Archambeault discusses in part 2. American Indian governments cannot protect them nor do their laws apply to them unless they come onto American Indian land. These protections are also hindered by the complicated nature of Indian Country and the many legal jurisdictions that affect it. *Indian Country* is a legal term used by authors in this and later sections of the book. It is defined as

> all land within the limits of any Indian reservation under the jurisdiction of the United States government, notwithstanding the issuance of any patent, and, including rights-of-way running through the reservation, (b) all dependent Indian communities within the borders of the United States whether within the original or subsequently acquired territory thereof, and whether within or without the limits of a state, and (c) all Indian allotments, the Indian titles to which have not been extinguished, including rights-of-way running through the same. (18 USCA §1151 1948)

The use of law as a means of control by the dominant society over time has hindered the ability of American Indian nations to protect their peoples against crimes of all types. A key aspect of Indigenous nation building and sovereignty is therefore using law to regain human rights and self-control of their nations by challenging discriminatory laws. This self-control is essential to the development of justice programs to resolve the many social and criminal justice issues they face daily. Some of the discriminatory laws, such as the Indian Major Crimes Act (1885) for example, restrict their ability to do so by limiting their jurisdiction to only minor crimes committed on reservations by American Indians, and limiting their ability to punish offenders. It should be noted that some seemingly pro-sovereignty laws, such as the Tribal Law and Order Act (2010), come with many expensive strings attached that make their provisions difficult to meet (see, for example, Archambeault 2014).

It is important to emphasize that Indigenous communities are asserting their sovereignty to develop programs designed to heal both Indigenous criminal offenders and victims of crimes, but they face obstacles such as the use of law to limit their authority. Sovereignty issues, therefore, relate closely to crime in Indigenous communities whether they are located on or off Indigenous lands.

REFERENCES

Archambeault, William G. 2014. The Current State of Indian Country Corrections in the United States. In *American Indians at Risk*, ed. Jeffrey Ian Ross, 77–93. Santa Barbara, CA: Greenwood.

Light, Steven A., and Kathryn A. L. Rand. 2005. *Indian Gaming and Tribal Sovereignty: The Casino Compromise*. Lawrence: University Press of Kansas.

Marshall, Gordon, ed. 1994. *Oxford Concise Dictionary of Sociology*. Oxford, UK: Oxford University Press.

Michalowski, Raymond J. 1985. *Order, Law, and Crime*. New York: Random House.

Sue, Derald Wing. 2010. Microaggressions, Marginality, and Oppression: An Introduction. In *Microaggressions and Marginality: Manifestation, Dynamics, and Impact*, ed. Derald Wing Sue, 3–22. Hoboken, NJ: John Wiley and Sons.

U.S. Census Bureau. 2012. "The American Indian and Alaska Native Population: 2010." Washington, D.C. http://www.census.gov/prod/cen2010/briefs/c2010br-10.pdf.

LEGAL SOURCES

Indian Gaming Regulatory Act (IGRA) PL 100-497 (1988)
Indian Major Crimes Act 18 U.S.C. § 1153 (1885)
Tribal Law and Order Act 25 U.S.C. 2801 (2010)
U.S. Code Annotated 18 USCA §1151 (1948)

1

ANOTHER TYPE OF HATE CRIME

Violence Against American Indian Women in Reservation Border Towns

CHERYL REDHORSE BENNETT

O N THE MORNING OF March 27, 2016, twenty-seven-year-old Loreal Tsingine was gunned down on the street by police officer Austin Shipley in Winslow, Arizona. Tsingine was a Navajo mother and daughter residing in the border town. It was reported that she was shoplifting at a convenience store and may have been intoxicated. After the store clerk called the police, Tsingine left the store. Shipley approached her, and Tsingine allegedly struggled and resisted arrest. Shipley claimed that she took out a pair of small scissors. Shipley then shot her five times and Tsingine died at the scene (Fonesca 2016).

Tsingine's murder resonated and shocked the Navajo and Winslow communities. Tsingine was a small Navajo woman, only five feet tall and approximately ninety-five pounds. Shipley was a very large white man with a questionable policing record including previous disciplinary action for excessive force (Jeong 2016). The Navajo Nation's response was immediate. The Navajo Nation president and Navajo Nation Council called for an investigation by U.S. Department of Justice attorney general Loretta Lynch into the shooting of Tsingine and "discriminatory practices of police officers racially profiling and targeting members of the tribe who live in nearby border towns" (Navajo Nation Council 2016, 2). The Navajo Nation Council (2016) also cited a concern for the "health, safety, and welfare of Navajos."

After Tsingine's killing, protests occurred in Winslow. Family members, activists, and the community demonstrated against her death and police violence. The Navajo community was outraged and argued that Shipley could have used a Taser or baton and was trained in subduing criminals. He did not need to shoot and kill Loreal Tsingine (Yazzie 2016). Shipley was initially put on administrative leave until the Winslow Police Department could investigate the shooting.

The Navajo community was even more shocked when the shooting was ruled as justified by the Maricopa County Attorney's Office. The Winslow Police Department released the body cam video taken from Shipley's camera. The footage showed Tsingine holding a pair of small scissors as she walked toward Shipley. After the video was released, the Winslow Police Department said that Shipley felt threatened and the use of force was justified. Austin Shipley maintained that he felt threatened by the small Navajo woman, and that is why he shot and killed her.

The Department of Justice announced that it would investigate the shooting of Tsingine. Additionally, Tsingine's family filed a $10.5 million civil lawsuit against the city of Winslow and Austin Shipley. The family claims that the city was negligent, in that Shipley had previous disciplinary action taken against him, other officers considered him emotional, and he had used excessive force in the past (Lartey 2016). One superior even recommended that the Winslow Police Department not retain Austin Shipley as a police officer.

Loreal Tsingine's death is not an isolated incident. This tragedy follows a historical pattern of violence toward American Indians in the United States, particularly women, and especially in reservation border towns. There has always been violence against American Indians by the police, but because of social media there is now slightly more attention given to this injustice. American Indians experience the most violence at the hands of police (Koerth-Baker 2016; Lakota People's Law Project n.d.). American Indian women are also incarcerated at a rate six times higher than are white women (Ross 1999). This violence is pervasive and continues a culture of oppression and colonialism.

Such violence is neither random nor new; in fact, it is a hate crime. There are varying definitions of hate crime, at both the federal and state level. State hate crime laws are used most often, whereas federal hate crime laws apply in the absence of state hate crime laws. Federal hate crime law covers race and sexual orientation. Violence and sexual assault against

American Indian women, especially in reservation border towns, should be viewed as a hate crime.

There is an added power dynamic to hate crimes committed against American Indians. Hate crimes have been used to assert power and to keep American Indians in their place, as an extension of colonization (Perry 2009). Using the term *hate crime* regarding violence against American Indian women demands attention. Tribal leaders, lawmakers, grassroots organizers, communities, and scholars all agree that violence against women is disproportionately high. The data back up this claim. Of all population groups, American Indian women have the highest rates of violence perpetrated against them (Deer 2015). Framing this violence around definitions of hate crime demonstrates that violence against women has in fact been a direct product of colonization and racism. American Indian women are targeted because of both their race and gender. In particular, this violence and hate crime happens in reservation border towns, as examined in this chapter.

THE RESERVATION BORDER TOWN

Since 2007, I have conducted research on reservation border towns and the racial violence that American Indians experience in these towns (Bennett 2013). The inspiration for conducting this type of research was due in large part to the disappearance of a high school friend. Further motivation for the need for this type of research, scholarship, and testimony occurred in 2007 when my father was undergoing a series of medical treatments in the neighboring border town of Farmington, New Mexico. The hospital staff treated my family poorly to the point of discrimination, and during hospital visits, I pondered the situation of Navajo and Native American people in relation to the border town of Farmington. This led to the decision to research and expose these issues, because there was a severe lack of academic scholarship that addressed violence in reservation border towns.

For the past six years, I have presented some of the findings of this work at various conferences and to the Navajo Nation.[1] A number of other scholars are now taking up the call for action and are engaging in this very difficult type of research. Reservation border towns have not been discussed in depth in academic literature. Chavers (2009), Perry (2009), and various government and tribal reports (NNHRC 2010; NMCCR 1975, 2005) bring attention to reservation border towns, but an in-depth analysis of the relationship American Indians have with border towns is lacking.

In previous research, I examined the racial dynamics in Farmington, New Mexico, and particularly border towns and found a predatory relationship with the neighboring Native populations, including in urban areas such as Phoenix, Denver, and Albuquerque (Bennett 2013). These cities are close to large populations of Native peoples but are large urban centers that may or may not be adjacent to the reservation.

The reservation border town is essentially an extension of the State and the colonizer. The settler inhabitants of the border town are direct beneficiaries of the legacy of colonization (Fanon 1968). The violence inflicted on American Indians has been discussed as an extension or another tool of colonization (Deer 2015; Smith 2005). Violence and hate crime are used as tools to assert control and power over American Indians. In border towns there is a sort of lawlessness regarding violence against American Indians. Border towns are places where whites can "get away with" harming American Indians. American Indians are viewed as a disposable population or annoyance in border towns. Additionally, there is a predatory nature to border towns. They are economically dependent on American Indians but do not actually want American Indians to be part of the community. As such, reservation border towns have been areas of violence against Native American women, especially in the areas of sexual violence and policing. The violence against women in border towns needs to be explored through the lens of colonization.

The question is not whether more violence occurs on the reservation or in border towns; it needs to be acknowledged that border towns are areas of frequent violence. The current focus of tribes and researchers is on violence that takes place in Indian Country, but violence at all levels needs to be addressed, in all areas. The argument is not being made that more violence against women occurs off-reservation; however, this pattern emerged during other research.

This chapter comes out of a concern regarding violence against American Indians in border towns but particularly women in border towns. American Indian men have also been frequent targets of violence in border towns, particularly in the form of hate crimes, murder, assault, and microaggressions (Bennett 2013). Women have been the targets of rape, physical assault, and murder. Most examples of this violence have been perpetrated by white males and other non-Indians. It is not being contended that white males or non-Indians perpetrate all the violence, but most violence perpetrated against American Indian women is by non-Indians. The literature supports this assertion (Deer 2015). It has been argued previously that this is not the situation on the Navajo Nation (Bennett 2010). In the Navajo example, Navajo men are the main perpetrators of violence against Navajo women; however, this does not mean that jurisdiction over non-Indians is not needed (Deer 2015).

OFF-RESERVATION SEXUAL ASSAULT OF AMERICAN INDIAN WOMEN

American Indian and Alaska Native women are sexually assaulted at a rate higher than women of other races. American Indian women are also stalked and have higher rates of domestic violence than women of other races. Numerous reports have shown this, including the *Maze of Injustice* report that demonstrated and documented the widespread sexual violence inflicted on American Indian and Alaska Native women in the United States. *Maze of Injustice* focused on American Indian women on reservations and "neighboring areas" (Amnesty International 2007). Many of the survivors who provide their testimony in the report are from border towns. Amnesty International surveyed three locations for their report: Standing Rock Sioux Reservation, the state of Oklahoma, and the state of Alaska.

Amnesty International (2007) argues that primarily white men perpetrate sexual violence against American Indians; however, there is an admitted lack of data and a great need for more research in this area. Enough sources, however, have concluded that violence against American Indian women by non-Indians is rampant. In reviewing the stories of survivors, there is an undeniable pattern that this violence by non-Indians happens frequently in reservation border towns:

> In Oklahoma, one support worker for Native American survivors of sexual violence told Amnesty International that 58 per cent of the cases she had worked on in the preceding 18 months involved non-Native perpetrators.

In Anchorage, Alaska, a statistical study found that 57.7 per cent of Alaska Native victims of sexual violence reported that their attackers had been non-Native men. (Amnesty International 2007, 5)

There is only one reservation in Oklahoma. The remainder of the Indian land is allotments, and although this makes it Indian Country (in the legal sense of the term), the jurisdictional maze in which it exists would essentially make all of Oklahoma a border town (Kemmick 2016).

Amnesty International also learned of many issues in Anchorage, which lies adjacent to many Alaska Native villages. Alaska Natives were more likely to be sexually assaulted in Anchorage, and "of the 41 confirmed cases in Alaska since 1991, 32 involved Alaska Native women" (Amnesty International 2007, 36).

Previously, much of the literature and focus has been on violence against American Indian women on reservations and in Indian Country. This is a very important focus since non-Indian perpetrators have found loopholes in the jurisdictional maze (Smith 2005). There are many cases where non-Native men raped or inflicted violence against American Indian women on reservations; even so, border towns also remain dangerous places for American Indian women.

American Indian women are a population at risk both on and off reservations. This is due to a long legacy of colonization. On reservations, the issue is a combination of jurisdictional issues, lack of policing, and in some cases culture loss (Bennett 2010). In border towns, the violence becomes commonplace due to long-standing discrimination and racism. Rape often goes unreported, and especially with American Indians, there is a long history of mistrust of the police and discriminatory practices by police, discussed later in this chapter, but the negative relationship with police—tribal, state, and city—leads to a lack of reporting out of a genuine fear of not being believed.

SEX TRAFFICKING AND PROSTITUTION IN BORDER TOWNS

Historically, sex trafficking went hand in hand with colonization: "Prostitution is another form of this egregious violence against Native women"

(Farley et al. 2011, 16). The first examples of sex trafficking occurred during the time of Columbus and later with the Spanish in California (Deer 2015). The fur trade also spurred sex trafficking when women were either kidnapped or sold into slavery. There is a long history of a slave trade in New Mexico, primarily targeting Navajo and Apaches, with women and girls attracting the highest prices. Some held in slavery risked their lives to escape from their captors (Broderick 1973). In some cases, Navajo women never made it back to their homes and families. After the Navajo returned from imprisonment at Bosque Redondo, Navajo people sought assistance to get their family members returned, but to no avail (Bennett 2013).

The legacy of trafficking is a continuation of this. Fortunately, sex trafficking in Indian Country is no longer a secret. There has been increasingly more research about this topic, including a call for more researchers to investigate this issue. Sex trafficking in Indian Country is a complicated problem. Drug addiction on some reservations has made sex trafficking more prevalent. Previously, what was known only as prostitution was more likely sex trafficking; often they are interconnected or the same thing (Deer 2015). In *Garden of Truth* (Farley et al. 2011), nearly half of the prostitutes interviewed said they were trafficked. Pimps lure girls off reservations in border areas (University of Minnesota 2014). According to the *Trafficking in Persons* report (U.S. Department of State 2016), Native Americans are a particularly vulnerable population. In recent years, the oil boom and subsequent creation of man camps in North Dakota has been cited as the cause of further sex trafficking of American Indian women and even children:

> That has been true in South Dakota, where the U.S. Attorney's Office has prosecuted sex trafficking cases involving several dozen victims. About half of those victims were American Indian women and girls. In most cases, the victimization did not occur on the reservations, but in Sioux Falls and other larger cities. (Dalrymple, 2015)

When at-risk American Indian women and girls leave the reservation, they are targeted by pimps and traffickers because they are without resources. Reservations are fraught with poverty, alcoholism, and broken homes, making American Indian women and girls an easy market for traffickers (Deer 2015).

Sex workers experience an added element of violence. The prostitutes interviewed in *Garden of Truth* (Farley et al. 2011) cite disturbing instances of violence and racism. Many described johns as having a fetish for American Indian women and having a stereotypical view of American Indian women that fuels their fetish. Out of the one hundred prostitutes interviewed, the majority reported that most of their clientele were white males and other non-Indians. The majority of them were also prostituted or trafficked in off-reservation areas, primarily Duluth and Minneapolis, as well as on ships in the Duluth harbor (Farley et al. 2011). They also experienced a greater level of physical violence and rape than prostitutes in other countries. Again, some of this was linked to legacies of colonization and stereotypes of American Indian women. One woman told the researchers, "A john said to me, 'I thought we killed all of you'" (Farley et al. 2011, 5).

In some areas there are a few organizations that could assist women seeking to escape from a life of trafficking. States and tribes are working together to help. Minnesota, a prime location for sex trafficking, has dedicated millions of dollars to curb trafficking (Women's Foundation of Minnesota n.d.). For example, the Minnesota Indian Women's Resource Center (n.d.) provides assistance to sex trafficking survivors. Billboards across the state of South Dakota campaign against trafficking (Sisters Against Trafficking 2016). It is important to remember that this is not just an Indian Country issue. Current federal trafficking laws can be enforced in and outside of Indian Country. Additionally, tribes can create their own human trafficking laws.

TRANSGENDER VIOLENCE

Transgender people, particularly transgender women, have often met with violence in reservation border towns. Transgender individuals have cited that they experience racism and discrimination, particularly in these areas (Incite! n.d.). In small reservation border towns such as Farmington, New Mexico, attitudes toward trans people and LGBTQ can be negative. In addition to the discrimination, racism, and violence toward American Indian populations, attitudes can also be hateful toward the LGBTQ community. Individuals who are both Native American and LGBTQ have stated that they have a very difficult life in reservation border towns, as seen in the following examples.

In 2001, Fred Martinez, a transgender Navajo youth, was killed in the border town of Cortez, Colorado. Shaun Murphy, a white Farmington, New Mexico, resident, bludgeoned Martinez to death when Martinez was walking home from a carnival. Murphy later bragged to friends he "bug smashed a fag." He was not charged with a hate crime but convicted of first-degree murder and sentenced to forty years in prison. Martinez's story was later memorialized in the documentary *Two Spirits* (Nibley 2009).[2] The film describes the murder as a transgender hate crime incident. But despite this differentiation, the Martinez murder was part of a larger pattern of ongoing violence against Navajos and American Indians in the Four Corners region. Martinez was doubly vulnerable because he was both transgender and a Navajo.

Transgender violence also occurs in urban border towns such as Phoenix. In many instances, the trans and gay community have had to watch or keep track of the violence and hate crimes targeting their community. Native Out (n.d.), a two-spirit educational and support website, documents several murdered transgender women and two-spirit individuals. These murders are often not investigated as hate crimes, yet gruesome and violent murders such as these have happened both in Phoenix and Albuquerque. The victims were from neighboring Phoenix tribes, including Gila River, Hopi, and Navajo. Today, these murders remain unsolved (Native Out n.d.).

AMERICAN INDIAN WOMEN AND POLICING

A young Navajo woman told me about an uncomfortable experience with a police officer in Farmington, New Mexico. Angie's[3] relative had been arrested at a retail store when Angie was underage. The officer had given Angie a ride home, and although she was not under arrest, she was told to ride in the back seat. The officer took a route through a remote part of Farmington and slowly pulled his car off to a dirt road. Angie began to get scared. Fortunately, another police car was driving by, and the officer immediately pulled back onto the main road and returned Angie home. She relayed this experience many years ago, raising the question of who else since then has experienced this sort of intimidation and even assault at the hands of police officers.

Although some areas have policing issues with reservation police officers, many times there are more issues with off-reservation policing and non-Indian police officers (Perry 2009) with altercations happening in reservation border towns. In 2011, Farmington police sergeant Kent O'Donnell was accused of raping a Navajo woman. The alleged victim claimed that she was probably not the first victim. There were other allegations that he had a pattern of harassing Navajo and Hispanic women in Farmington. O'Donnell was placed on administrative leave while the woman's allegation was investigated. The alleged victim also filed a complaint with the Farmington Community Relations Board, saying that the accusation was not being taken seriously. No charges were filed against O'Donnell, though he is no longer a police officer and runs a tactical training company in the Phoenix metro area.

Native American people are more likely than any other race or ethnic group to be killed by police ("The Counted" 2015):

> Native women and Native Two Spirit, transgender, and gender nonconforming people are subjected to gender-specific forms of law enforcement violence, such as racial profiling, physical abuse, sexual harassment and abuse, and failure to respond or abusive responses to reports of violence. (Incite! n.d.)

According to the *Guardian*, Native Americans have the highest percentage of shootings by police according to population size ("The Counted" 2015). This is especially evident with transgender individuals and in relation to human trafficking and sex workers. Oftentimes in these instances, there is an additional layer of police harassment and intimidation. For example, in an episode of the television show *Cops*, a Navajo transwoman was stopped by Albuquerque police for loitering. She was not gender identified correctly and mocked by police ("Cross Dresser Arrested" 2010). Trans people have a history of mistreatment by police. They have often been targets of further violence, intimidation, and even rape. Again, more often these apprehensions and police encounters are happening in reservation border towns and urban border towns (Amnesty International 2005).

During the past few years, the Native Lives Matter[4] movement has brought awareness to police brutality in Rapid City and other areas in South Dakota. Chase Iron Eyes of People's Law Project leads the movement. The Lakota People's Law Project (n.d.) also authored a report, *Native Lives Matter*, that delves into police misconduct in South Dakota, including the shooting of a Native Lives Matter protester and an eight-year-old Lakota girl stun gunned by police. Native Lives Matter has actively demonstrated and protested in Rapid City to fight against police brutality. But despite their effort, the Native Lives Matter movement has not garnered as much attention or interest as other social justice movements. The issue of American Indians and police brutality has still gone relatively unnoticed by the general public.

MISSING AND MURDERED AMERICAN INDIAN WOMEN

I spent my childhood in the border town of Kirtland, New Mexico, a small community outside of Farmington. In 1988, this small community was shaken by the murder of a young Navajo woman, Marlene Tsosie Wilson. White teenager Chad Freeman and his accomplice Jimmy Guiterez stabbed Wilson in the chest, attempting to cut out her heart. Both perpetrators were non-Indian and served minimal time. Guiterez was sentenced to serve a few years in a juvenile facility and Freeman was sentenced as an adult. During the murder trial, the focus was on the possible link to satanic cults and the gruesome details of the crime. National attention to this horrific crime was scant, if not nonexistent. Even now, it's difficult to find any information on the perpetrators, one of whom only served about three years in a juvenile facility before returning to Kirtland (McCutcheon 1988, 50).

This case was one of many that occurred during this time. For example, on February 1, 1995, Sadie Frost and Shawnda Baker were found in a parked car on a rural road west of Durango, Colorado. Frost had been shot in the head and was deceased. Baker was also shot in the head but was still alive. Raymond Cain and Gabriel Rivera, both non-Indian, shot the women, apparently to rob them of the per capita payment they received when they had turned eighteen years of age. Cain and Rivera were both sentenced in the murder of Frost and attempted murder of Baker. The motive for this crime was cited as robbery, but there was an added element of anti-Indianism by targeting Frost and Baker because they were American Indian (Benjamin 2016).

In 1980, Candace Rough Surface's remains were discovered outside Mobridge, South Dakota. The crime was horrific; she was raped, shot, and dragged behind a truck to be dumped. Rough Surface was from the Standing Rock Reservation. Nearly fifteen years after her murder, two white men from Mobridge were arrested. James Stroh and Nicholas Scherr confessed to the crime and claimed that Rough Surface approached them in a bar wanting sex, insinuating that Rough Surface was promiscuous. They gave her a ride to a house party and murdered her. Stroh was sentenced to fifteen years in prison, eligible for parole after eighteen months. Scherr was sentenced to one hundred years for manslaughter and is eligible for parole in 2017 (Associated Press 1996). This crime shocked the small border town of Mobridge and ignited long-standing racial tensions between the communities. The white community circulated a petition to have the perpetrators released, indicating their dismissive attitude toward the murder of Rough Surface. The Standing Rock community believed that the police would have investigated more thoroughly if she were white (Wronski 1996). In all these horrible crimes, white men were mostly the perpetrators and the crimes occurred in border towns. There was little media attention to these killings, and the non-Indian community was apathetic.

When looking for ways to ameliorate the propensity of violence against American Indian women in border towns, it is necessary to look at the root causes of the violence. In all the instances of violence against American Indian women, there are stereotypes involved.

This issue is not restricted to the United States. The outrageous numbers of missing and murdered Indigenous women in Canada has been an ongoing problem for years. In 1971, Helen Betty Osborne was murdered in The Pas, a town bordering a Manitoba reserve (Acoose 1995). Four white men kidnapped, raped, beat, and murdered her. There had been reports in The Pas about white men cruising town looking for Aboriginal girls to drink with and use for sex. Sixteen years later, only one of the men had been brought to justice. The murder of and lack of justice for Osborne, along with the Royal Canadian Mounted Police shooting of a tribal leader, led to the creation of the Aboriginal Justice Inquiry Commission. The commission conducted hearings and filed a report detailing their findings, which included that stereotypes of First Nations women directly led to violence and sexual violence (Hamilton and Sinclair 1991). In the United States, stereotypes of American Indian women as drunks and promiscuous have also led to the violence perpetrated against them.

CONCLUSION

Since Tsingine's death there have been a variety of protests, demonstrations, and calls for further investigations. Particularly, there has been action on the part of the Navajo Nation and the Navajo Nation Human Rights Commission (NNHRC). The NNHRC surveyed and called for testimony about violence against Navajo women, but it remains unclear what effect, if any, the NNHRC has had on border town relations and violence. The NNHRC has come under criticism in the past from the Navajo Nation Council for not improving race relations in border towns. It will take a multilevel approach to address this monumental issue of violence against Native American women in border towns.

Other efforts have been made; for example, in 2011, the State Department visited the Navajo Nation, gathering information on the state of race relations. The testimony they received included information about Winslow, Arizona, where there had been a number of unattended deaths that the Navajo community from Winslow was concerned about. No follow-up came out of the State Department meeting. In fact, the criticism from the Navajo community about the State Department's visit reached the point where community members stated that they did not expect anything to come of that meeting.

If the violence against American Indian women is looked at as a hate crime, then some of the hate crime prevention tactics that have proven effective in other communities could be implemented. This is not to preclude the gains that have been made in the reauthorization of the Violence Against Women Act, or the creation of the Tribal Law and Order Act, but it has been shown in other communities that have been fraught with hate crime that educational, legal, and community efforts have made a marked difference.

Additionally, American Indian nations and communities need to take an aggressive stance against violence against American Indian women that takes place in border towns. The Navajo Nation's example of this is admirable. They were unwavering in their support of Loreal Tsingine's family. Communities have also taken it upon themselves to guard their own people. For example, in Winnipeg, Canada, a group of citizens called the Bear Clan patrols the border city of Winnipeg. This has been in response to a rash of murders, in particular the murder of a young girl, Tina Fontaine, who was wrapped in a plastic bag and found in a river. The group seeks to protect women and children and has been active since 2014.

In addition to the ongoing efforts to combat violence against American Indian women, communities should also confront this violence as hate crime. Previously, non-Indian communities have dealt with hate crimes in a variety of ways. These groups have tried interventions and have seen improvement. Part of the strategy of non-Indian organizations' advocacy efforts is to educate and bring awareness about hate crimes in order to prevent them. Other racial and ethnic groups have had success through educational campaigns and awareness-raising initiatives. Advocacy groups such as the Southern Poverty Law Center have had some measured success in lawsuits against organizations such as the Aryan Nations by asserting civil rights violations by these groups. The Southern Poverty Law Center's mission is to seek justice while fighting hate; its educational initiative is called Teaching Tolerance (n.d.). The center's educational materials and teacher training on hate crimes are offered to schools and communities. Perry (2009) argues for education at the K–12 school level and modeling the Anti-Defamation League's education on antihate programs in order to curb racist attitudes and the stereotypes that fuel negative perceptions of American Indian people and women in particular. This would be particularly beneficial in border towns.

Largely due to social media and the new growth in American Indian media sources, violence against American Indian women does not go as undocumented and hidden as it has in the past. For example, the grassroots organization Save Wiyabi has been very active in documenting missing and murdered Indigenous women in the United States. Unfortunately, there has not been as intensive an effort as seen in Canada to document the missing and murdered women. The cofounder of Save Wiyabi stated that they discovered that sometimes the tribal identity of missing women was ignored (Chief Elk 2014). The blog and mapping effort of the website Justice for Native Women (n.d.) brings attention to the invisible issue of the missing and murdered Native women from North America. A non-Indian former homicide detective created a website called Lost and Missing in Indian Country (n.d.) and works with American Indian advocates to solve missing persons cases. In large part, American Indian women and Indigenous women are those doing this important work documenting the missing and murdered. They are at the forefront of this call for action.

This issue has garnered major attention in the last ten years, but the numbers remain the same. American Indian women still have the highest rates of violence perpetrated against them. The examples provided within this chapter are only a small sampling of the violence perpetrated daily against American Indian women in the United States. There are no simple answers to ending the scourge of violence against American Indian women. It will take generations to heal the damage that hundreds of years of colonization have done to American Indian and other Indigenous women.

NOTES

1. Western Social Sciences Association, American Indian Studies Association, Navajo Nation IRB, and Northern Agency Council.

2. *Two spirit* is "a generic term for Native American gays, lesbians, transgendered individuals, and other persons who are not heterosexual or who are ambivalent in terms of gender, it is used in urban and rural environments, but not by all Native Americans," according to Jacobs, Thomas, and Lang (1997, 3).

3. Her name has been changed to protect her privacy.

4. The co-opting of this term from the Black Lives Matter movement has been controversial, and some Native activists argue against using it.

REFERENCES

Acoose, Janice. 1995. *Iskwewak—Kah' Ki Yaw Ni Wahkomakanak: Neither Indian Princess Nor Easy Squaw.* Toronto, ON: Women's Press.

Amnesty International. 2005. *Stonewalled: Police Abuse and Misconduct Against Lesbian, Gay, Bisexual and Transgender People in the U.S.* New York: Author. https://www.amnesty.org/en/documents/AMR51/122/2005/en/.

————. 2007. *Maze of Injustice: The Failure to Protect Indigenous Women From Sexual Violence in the USA*. New York: Author. http://www.amnestyusa.org/pdfs /MazeOfInjustice.pdf.

Associated Press. 1996. "100-Year Term in Sioux's Rape and Murder." *New York Times*, May 23. http://www.nytimes.com/1996/05/23/us/100-year-term-in -sioux-s-rape-and-murder.html.

Benjamin, Shane. 2016. "Man Convicted of '95 Murder to Be Resentenced in Durango." *Durango Herald*. https://durangoherald.com/articles/109552-man -convicted-of-x2019-95-murder-to-be-resentenced-in-durango.

Bennett, Cheryl Redhorse. 2010. *Against Tradition: Violence Against Navajo Women*. Santa Barbara, CA: ABC-CLIO.

————. 2013. "Investigating Hate Crimes in Farmington, N.M." PhD diss., University of Arizona.

Broderick, Johnson, ed. 1973. *Navajo Stories of the Long Walk*. Tsaile: Navajo Community College Press.

Chavers, Dean. 2009. *Racism in Indian Country*. New York: Peter Lang.

Chief Elk, Lauren. 2014. "The Missing Women You Don't Hear About: How the Media Fails Indigenous Communities." *Salon*, February 14. http://www .salon.com/2014/02/14/the_missing_women_you_dont_hear_about_how_the _media_fails_indigenous_communities.

"The Counted." 2015. *The Guardian*. https://www.theguardian.com/us-news/ng -interactive/2015/jun/01/the-counted-police-killings-us-database.

"Cross Dresser Arrested—Excuse My Beauty." 2010. YouTube. https://www.you-tube.com/watch?v=jSiIirICPwo.

Dalrymple, Amy. 2015. "Native American Population 'Hugely at Risk' to Sex Trafficking." *Bismarck Tribune*, January 5. http://bismarcktribune.com/bakken /native-american-populations-hugely-at-risk-to-sex-trafficking/article _46511e48-92c5-11e4-b040-c7db843de94f.html.

Deer, Sarah. 2015. *The Beginning and End of Rape: Confronting Sexual Violence in Native America*. Minneapolis: University of Minnesota Press.

Fanon, Frantz. 1968. *The Wretched of the Earth*. New York: Grove Press.

Farley, Melissa, Nicole Matthews, Sarah Deer, Guadalupe Lopez, Christine Stark, and Eileen Hudon. 2011. *Garden of Truth: The Prostitution and Trafficking of Native Women in Minnesota*. Saint Paul, MN: William Mitchell College of Law.

Fonesca, Felicia. 2016. "Police: Woman Killed by Winslow AZ Officer Held Scissors." *AZ Central*, March 9. http://www.azcentral.com/story/news/local /arizona/2016/03/29/police-woman-killed-winslow-arizona-officer-held -scissors/82406706/.

Hamilton, A. C., and C. M. Sinclair. 1991. *Report of the Aboriginal Justice Inquiry of Manitoba: The Deaths of Helen Betty Osborne and John Joseph Harper*. Winnipeg, Manitoba: Province of Manitoba. http://www.ajic.mb.ca/volume.html.

Jacobs, Sue-Ellen, Wesley Thomas, and Sabine Lang. 1997. *Two-Spirited People*. Urbana: University of Illinois Press.

Jeong, Yihun. 2016. "7 Facts to Know About the Winslow Shooting." *AZ Central*, August 3. http://www.azcentral.com/story/news/local/arizona/2016/08/03/7 -facts-know-winslow-shooting-loreal-tsingine/87935232/.

Justice for Native Women. n.d. http://justicefornativewomen.blogspot.com/.

Incite! n.d. http://www.incite-national.org/.

Kemmick, Ed. 2016. "'All of Montana Is a Border Town' Civil Rights Panel Told." *Last Best News*, August 3. http://lastbestnews.com/site/2016/08/all-of -montana-is-a-border-town-civil-rights-panel-told/.

Koerth-Baker, Maggie. 2016. "Police Violence Against Native Americans Goes Far Beyond Standing Rock." *FiveThirtyEight*, December 2. https://fivethirty eight.com/features/police-violence-against-native-americans-goes-far -beyond-standing-rock/.

Lakota People's Law Project. n.d. "Native Lives Matter." https://s3-us-west-1 .amazonaws.com/lakota-peoples-law/uploads/Native-Lives-Matter-PDF.pdf.

Lartey, Jamiles. 2016. "Justice Department Investigating Fatal Police Shooting of Loreal Tsingine." *The Guardian*, July 30. https://www.theguardian.com/usnews /2016/jul/30/native-american-police-deaths-loreal-tsingine.

Lost and Missing in Indian Country. n.d. http://lostandmissinginindiancountry .com.

McCutcheon, Chuck. 1988. "Fruitland Teen Faces Trial as Adult." *Albuquerque Journal*, December 8, p. 55.

Native Out: Native American and Two-Spirit Educational Resources. n.d. http:// nativeout.com/.

Navajo Nation Council. 2016. Legislation No. 0137–16, 2.

Navajo Nation Human Rights Commission. 2010. *Assessing Race Relations in Navajo Nation Bordertowns*. Window Rock: Navajo Nation. http://www.nnhrc .navajo-nsn.gov/docs/NewsRptResolution/071810%20Assessing%20Race %20Relations%20Between%20Navajos%20and%20Non-Navajos.pdf.

New Mexico Advisory Committee to the U.S. Commission on Civil Rights. 1975. *The Farmington Report*. Washington, D.C.: U.S. Commission on Civil Rights. https://www.law.umaryland.edu/marshall/usccr/documents/cr12f222.pdf.

———. 2005. *The Farmington Report: Civil Rights for Native Americans 30 Years Later*. Washington, D.C.: U.S. Commission on Civil Rights. http://www.usccr .gov/pubs/122705_FarmingtonReport.pdf.

Nibley, Lydia. *Two Spirits*. 2009. DVD. Los Angeles: Riding the Tiger Productions.

Perry, Barbara. 2009. *Silent Victims*. Tucson: University of Arizona Press.

Minnesota Indian Women's Resource Center. n.d. https://www.miwrc.org/.

Ross, Luana. 1999. *Inventing the Savage: The Social Construction of Native American Criminality*. Austin: University of Texas Press.

Sisters Against Trafficking. 2016. "South Dakota Sisters Are Fighting Human Trafficking." Arts and Creative Activism Awareness. http://www.sistersagainst trafficking.org/2016/03/07/south-dakota-sisters-fighting-human-trafficking/.

Smith, Andrea. 2005. *Conquest: Sexual Violence and American Indian Genocide*. Boston: South End Press.

Teaching Tolerance. n.d. http://www.tolerance.org/.

University of Minnesota. 2014. *Mapping the Market for Sex with Trafficked Minor Girls in Minneapolis: Structures, Functions, and Patterns*. http://uroc.umn.edu /sites/default/files/MTM_SexTraf_Summ.pdf.

U.S. Department of State. 2016. *Trafficking in Person Report*. Washington, D.C.: Author. https://www.state.gov/documents/organization/258876.pdf.

Women's Foundation of Minnesota. n.d. "Minnesota Girls Are Not for Sale." http://www.wfmn.org/mn-girls-are-not-for-sale/.

Wronski, Richard. 1996. "16-Year Murder Mystery Ends in Tears." *Chicago Tribune*, July 2. http://www.articles.chicagotribune.com/1996-07-02/news/9607020074 _1_missouri-river-candace-rough-surface-first-degree-manslaughter.

Yazzie, Duane Chili. 2016. "Police Should Reevaluate Use of Force." *Daily Times*, August 6. http://www.dailytimes.com/story/opinion/readers/2016/08/06 /letters-readers-weigh-issues-day/88317962/.

LEGAL RESOURCES

Tribal Law and Order Act 25 U.S.C. 2801 (2010).

Violence Against Women Act 42 U.S.C. 13701 (1994, 2000, 2005, 2013).

2

STERILIZATION OF AMERICAN INDIAN WOMEN REVISITED

Another Attempt to Solve the "Indian Problem"

LINDA M. ROBYN

WHY REVISIT THE sterilization of American Indian women? This is an issue from the past, right? Wrong. The colonial context of coerced sterilization is not only part of the history of African American, Hispanic, Puerto Rican, American Indian, and Alaska Native women but also includes Indigenous women from Canada, Australia, and New Zealand. Coerced sterilization, however, is not included in much of the literature written about Indigenous women from these (and other) countries. It is important for people to be informed about the impact of colonialism and how it created historical trauma, historical oppression, and structural oppression in marginalized communities. Gender roles changed under colonialism, and coerced sterilizations performed on Indigenous women are part of the constellation of marginalization and discrimination experienced in tribes and communities. The physical results of forced sterilizations and abortions heal, but mentally, many women endure untreated post-traumatic stress syndrome for the rest of their lives.

Another reason it is important to learn about and revisit the sterilization practices that many Indigenous women were forced to endure is because *they are still happening* in some countries. In many parts of the world, women have access to various methods of birth control, including voluntary sterilization. However, sometimes sterilization is not a choice. In Australia, sterilization of Aboriginal women and children was and is widespread. Jabour (2015) writes that Australia's human rights record is being assessed by the United Nations Human Rights Council to review sterilization of children and women with mental and physical disabilities. Children cannot give consent because they are minors, and "Australia does not have any laws in place to prohibit the forced sterilization of women with disabilities, or children, and it falls under the UN definition of torture" (Jabour 2015, 2). One example cited by Jabour (2015, 3) is a thirty-nine-year-old woman who was sterilized when she was seven years old because she had a vision impairment.

In New Zealand, female reformers, colonial feminists, and welfare workers participated in debates about eugenics of "mental defectives" and "sexual offenders" and the role of women as both agents and subjects of eugenics (Wanhalla 2007). Eugenics fit the colonial ideals of the time surrounding racial health. In these debates, it was determined that sterilization as a eugenic solution would be reserved for "deviant women," and white middle-class female reformers, health professionals, and colonial feminists would take on the role of "mothers of the race" (Wanhalla 2007).

Aboriginal women in Canada experienced coercive sterilization for much the same reason as Native American women: to separate people from their lands and resources and to reduce the number of people on welfare. The coercive sterilization of women in Canadian health centers during the 1970s targeted impoverished communities disproportionately to lessen the state's responsibilities under treaties it had signed with Indigenous groups (Arsenault 2015). As with Native American women, 1,200 sterilizations (more than 550 at federally operated "Indian" hospitals) from 1972 to 1974 were performed by force, coercion, or fraud, and evidence suggests coercion was widespread (Stote quoted in Arsenault 2015). As with other women (and men) in impoverished communities, eugenics and the idea of racial superiority also played a part in reducing certain traits from the population (Arsenault 2015).

In the United States, the state has played a very important role in the history of female reproductive health. Disproportionate numbers of lower-class women and women of color were targeted for sterilization to control their population. Sterilizing women who fell into these categories would ensure the elimination of, or at least a great reduction in, people of color that were deemed to be a burden on taxpayers through the welfare system. Sterilization without consent is important to revisit because of the tragic breech of medical ethics that took place in the United States with forced sterilization from 1909 through 1979, subsidized through federal funding (Stern 2005). Also, a significant number of these sterilizations occurred *after* the Nuremberg trials (see Churchill 1997, 363–98). These trials are important to note because the United States took a leadership role regarding "crimes against humanity" under which genocidal policies and practices were prosecuted (Smith quoted in Churchill 1997, 364). Another reason to revisit sterilization of Native Americans (and other women of color) is the erosion of the Hippocratic oath stating the proper conduct of physicians that runs through every aspect of this tragedy and reminds us of the danger in separating ethical conviction from medical care. An expert on medical law and ethics, Marc Hiller states that "informed consent reflects one of our highest ethical values—individual autonomy; it implicates strong emotional needs both for control over our own lives and for dependence upon others; and it deals with a subject of fundamental importance, our health" (Relf et al. 1974, 1201). This is the context for state policy in the not too distant past toward the sterilization of American Indian women.

BACKGROUND

Although total genocide of Native Americans was impossible in the 1960s and 1970s, sterilization presented another form of elimination or, at the very least, population control of "undesirable" populations. The stage was set for using sterilization as a method of population control through the history and wide acceptance of eugenics in the twentieth century. Eugenics, practiced early in the twentieth century, was brought to life once again in the 1960s and 1970s and practiced through "voluntary physician complicity" on a national scale (Rutecki 2010, n.p.). Knowingly limiting births in selected populations was "emblematic of eugenics policy in the early to mid-twentieth century" (Rutecki 2010, n.p.).

Harry Laughlin (1880–1943) was a leading American eugenicist during the first half of the twentieth century and acted as superintendent of the Eugenics Record Office from its inception in 1910 until 1939. Laughlin actively influenced American eugenics, especially compulsory sterilization. As superintendent of the Eugenics Record Office in 1914, he published a model eugenical sterilization law that proposed sterilization of "socially inadequate" people who either lived in institutions or were supported by welfare. Laughlin's list included the "feebleminded, criminalistic, epileptic, inebriate, diseased, blind, deaf, deformed and dependent"—including "orphans, ne'er-do-wells, tramps, the homeless and paupers" (Laughlin 1926, 64–65). By the time the model law passed in 1914, twelve states had enacted sterilization laws.

New theories such as "eugenics, genetics, statistics and intelligence tests were used to buttress entrenched prejudices" (Reynolds 2005, 29). People who bought into the notion of the eugenics movement concluded that society would be improved for the fit and intelligent and that it would prevent those regarded as "undesirables" from breeding, even if it meant sterilization of various populations (Reynolds 2005, 58). This "new biological revelation" would result in "superior stocks," allowing people to "bridge political gulfs, remedy social abuses and exorcise the 'lurking spectre of miscegenation'" (Reynolds 2005, 66). During this period, the belief was that "undesirable traits such as poverty, mental illness, homosexuality, and promiscuity were inheritable traits that could be passed down to offspring and 'corrupt' future generations" (Sloan, Weischedel, and Yasen 2010, n.p.).

SCIENTIFIC RACISM AND STERILIZATION

During the nineteenth and twentieth centuries, scientific racism reached great heights, leading to the notion that groups with certain "defects" should be subject to methods of population control. This was demonstrated by the mainstream scientific community through "physical anthropology, craniometry, phrenology, eugenics, physiognomy, and other disciplines concerned with the classification of humans into distinct races and racial categories" (Echo-Hawk 2010, 249). People who fit these categories were believed to have innate traits "such as intelligence, morals, habits, and the capacity for civilization." Findings from the scientific community "supported master-race ideologies, and their theories postulated notions of racial superiority—the scientific community provided the world with scientific support for popular racism of the day" (Echo-Hawk 2010, 249).

With the eugenics movement in motion, sterilizations took place in our country from the late 1920s through the late 1930s among African

American and Puerto Rican women in an effort to control their population and poverty. As early as 1907, the United States instituted public policy that gave the government the right "to sterilize unwilling and unwitting people" (Krase 2014, n.p.). If the lynching of blacks can be viewed as a form of genocide, targeting women of color for involuntary sterilization is comparable.

With information from the mainstream scientific community, women of color were caught up in a "legitimate" effort to control the population. African American, Hispanic, Puerto Rican, and Native American women were sterilized during seemingly innocuous visits to physicians. Young women undergoing appendectomies or tonsillectomies were sterilized during the procedures. Women who had cesarean sections were never told before the sterilization took place; others were threatened with termination of welfare benefits or denial of medical benefits if they did not consent to the procedures; still others received unnecessary hysterectomies at teaching hospitals as practice for medical residents. In the South, sterilization was such a widespread practice that it had a euphemism: a "'Mississippi appendectomy'" (Wade 2011, n.p.).

Churchill (1997) writes that in the 1950s there was discussion in the African American community about involuntary sterilization and cites a 240-page petition written by black attorney William L. Patterson for the American Civil Rights Congress (CRC) titled "We Charge Genocide." This document was given to the UN secretariat in New York and in great detail documented sterilization programs to which the African American community had been subjected. By 1970, an updated version of the CRC petition was given to the UN secretariat that was even more sensitive. The U.S. government was continuing its "birth control efforts" with blacks and had secretly started with Native Americans and Puerto Ricans, resulting in approximately 30 percent of women in each group being sterilized (Churchill 1997, 376, 377).

Along with these historical sterilization practices affecting African American, Native American, and Puerto Rican women are more current sterilization practices for women prisoners. Four California prisons illegally sterilized thirty-nine women from fiscal years 2005–2006 to 2012–2013, with nearly one-third of those performed without lawful consent; for example, the inmate's physician would perform the procedure in a hospital but fail to sign a form stating the patient was of sound mind and understood the permanence of this operation (Nicholson 2014, n.p.). In addition, eighteen of the thirty-nine women were not notified of the required waiting period before the procedure was performed (Nicholson 2014). "According to California state law, sterilization can only be carried out between 30 and 180 days from the time a woman agrees to the procedure to provide the patient with enough time to reflect on her choice and to make sure she desires sterilization" (Nicholson 2014, n.p.). In addition, auditors found that in many cases "less than a week elapsed between the date of the request and the date of the surgery" (Nicholson 2014, n.p.). And, on another disconcerting note, the auditors found that, in some cases, physicians changed the dates on the forms to show that the necessary waiting period had expired even though it had not.

Auditors reported that "the true number of illegal procedures might be higher, noting that it had found seven cases at one hospital for which health records were lost in a routine purging . . . and auditors have called on federal officials to forward the names of the physicians involved in the illegal surgeries to the Medical Board and the California Department of Public Health for further investigation and disciplinary action" (Nicholson 2014, n.p.). It is important to look at sterilization of women prisoners without proper consent because we do not know who these women were. How many were African American, Native American, Hispanic, or Puerto Rican in this example of the government reducing the population of what authorities consider "undesirable people"?

COURT RULINGS ON STERILIZATION

Court rulings played an important role in federal family planning policies that had an influence on Indian Health Service (IHS) family planning programs between 1914 and 1973 (Lawrence 2000, 403). The U.S. Supreme Court set legal precedent regarding sterilization in the case of *Scholendorff v. Society of New York Hospital* in 1914. That year a surgeon performed an operation on a man that left him partially paralyzed. The U.S. Supreme Court stated that "any person who physically touches another individual without that person's consent commits battery" (Hiller 1981, 198). Justice Benjamin Cardoza stated that "every human being of adult years and sound mind has a right to determine what shall be done with his own body; and a surgeon who performs an operation without his patient's consent commits an assault" (Hiller 1981, 198). In the 1942 case of *Skinner v. Oklahoma*, the U.S. Supreme Court heard arguments of Jack Skinner, an inmate in an Oklahoma prison following his third offense of armed robbery. Oklahoma passed legislation allowing habitual criminals to be sterilized. In 1942, many states were already sterilizing people because, as mentioned previously, the eugenics movement advocated sterilization for the "unfit" (Lawrence 2000, 404). Justice William Douglas wrote the majority ruling stating Skinner's crime did not merit sterilization and declared "that the Oklahoma sterilization law was unconstitutional under the Fourteenth Amendment and expressed concern over the possibility of sterilization abuse arising from such legislation." He stated that "the power to sterilize, if exercised, may have far-reaching and devastating effects . . . [and in] evil hands it can cause races or types which are inimical to the dominant group to wither and disappear" (Lawrence 2000, 404; see also Hall 1992, 788; and Weisbord 1975, 139).

These cases are about the issue of informed consent and a patient's right to make an informed decision about what can be done to his or her body. With Native women, doctors did not fully disclose the nature and purpose of sterilization, the risks involved, or alternative treatments. The highest ethical value of informed consent was absent in the sterilization of Native women.

THE STERILIZATION OF
NATIVE AMERICAN WOMEN

Imagine two images of Native American women. One is the Disney portrayal of an exotic and beautiful *Indian princess* who leaves her society to ride off into the sunset with her handsome European American man. Now imagine the *squaw*. Her image suggests an Indian woman who has a problem with alcohol, lives in filthy conditions, neglects her children, and is not capable of the same human emotions as white women. She needs to repent her sins, be cleansed, and consequently be sterilized so as not to pass down her traits to even more children. *Sterilization racism* is defined as the organization of racist controlling images, policies, and practices of delivering reproductive health care that operate to constrain, minimize, or eliminate the reproductive activities of women of color (Neubeck and Cazenave 2001, 288). Given racist attitudes toward

African American, Puerto Rican, Hispanic, and Native American women living in poverty conditions and on welfare, the only qualifying attribute that matters is the color of her skin.

Along with African American and Puerto Rican women, Native American women were one of the most heavily targeted groups by the United States compulsory sterilization policy. Reports of coercive, involuntary sterilizations without consent began to surface in the United States during an intense time of civil rights activity; Native American and African American women and girls were especially impacted by sterilization abuse (Volscho 2010, 17). Institutionalized sterilization through use of coercion pushed women toward hysterectomy or tubal ligation, that is, "tying the tubes." Coercive tactics were used by physicians and others denying women access to informed consent, and the phrase "tying the tubes" led women to believe the surgery could be reversed (Krase 2014, n.p.).

These tactics were also used on Native American women who were seen for centuries as being dependent and not capable of overseeing their own affairs. If Natives were not capable of handling their own affairs, it was no great leap for the government to assume they were not capable of regulating their own reproductive rights. Therefore, legitimizing sterilization of Native American women was just another method leading to exploitation and taking care of the "Indian problem" in the United States. Native women were subjected to coercive population control practices through much of the twentieth century (Krase 2014, n.p.).

In 1965, authority was given to IHS and Health Education and Welfare (HEW) to provide family planning services for Native Americans to give women information on different methods of birth control, how the methods work, and how to use them (Lawrence 2000, 402). The United States government agency personnel, including IHS, targeted Native Americans for family planning because of their high birth rate. In 1970, the average birth rate for white women was 2.42 children and lowered to 2.14 in 1980 compared to 1.99 for Native American communities. Howard, Thornton, and Tiller concluded this discrepancy may be due to higher levels of education among Native women, along with family planning programs, but that sterilization as a partial cause of the decline must be considered as a factor (Lawrence 2000, 402).

Coercive tactics included hysterectomies, which are not common in young women of childbearing age unless there is cancer or other medical problems. One of many examples of this kind of abuse was a young Indian woman who went to see Dr. Connie Pinkerton-Uri in her Los Angeles office to ask for a "womb transplant." The twenty-six-year-old woman and her husband wanted to start a family. Upon further investigation, Dr. Pinkerton-Uri discovered that "an Indian Health Service (IHS) physician had given the woman a complete hysterectomy when she was having problems with alcoholism six years earlier. Dr. Pinkerton-Uri had to give the young woman the devastating news that there was no such thing as a womb transplant and that her surgery was irreversible" (Lawrence 2000, 400).

In another tragic incident, two young women entered an IHS hospital in Montana for appendectomies. In addition to the appendectomies, the young women also received tubal ligations as "an added benefit" (Lawrence 2000, 400). Bertha Medicine Bull of the Northern Cheyenne tribe recalled how these two young women "had been sterilized at age fifteen before they had any children. Both were having appendectomies when the doctors sterilized them without their knowledge or consent; their parents were not informed either" (Miller, Miller, and Szechenyl 1978, 423). One can only imagine the heartbreak these young women and their families endured.

Sterilizing Native Americans was not an uncommon occurrence for young women entering IHS hospitals in the 1960s and 1970s. Native Americans have accused IHS of sterilizing at least 25 percent of women between the ages of 15 and 44 (Lawrence 2000). Dr. Connie Pinkerton-Uri, a Choctaw-Cherokee physician, has been a pioneer in exposing forced sterilizations among Native American women. In 1974, she conducted a study that predicted 25,000 Native American women would be sterilized by 1975. Pinkerton-Uri found that IHS facilities singled out full-blood Native women for sterilization procedures. Pinkerton-Uri stated that "we have only 100,000 women of child-bearing age total—that's not per anything. The Indian population of this country is dwindling no matter what government statistics say to the contrary" (Lawrence 2000, 412). She discovered that Native women usually agreed to consent of sterilization when they were threatened with the loss of children they already had and loss of welfare benefits. Most gave consent while they were heavily sedated, in a great deal of pain while in labor, and signed consent forms they could not understand because the forms were written in English at the twelfth-grade level (Lawrence 2000, 411, 412).

In 1973, the Department of Health, Education, and Welfare (HEW) published regulations in the *Federal Register* that IHS had to follow. HEW placed a moratorium on the sterilization of anyone under the age of twenty-one and on anyone doctors declared mentally incompetent. The regulations stated that competent individuals must give their informed consent, that there must be a signed consent form in the possession of the agency performing the sterilization showing that the patient knew the benefits and costs of sterilizations, and that a seventy-two-hour waiting period must occur between time of consent and the surgical procedure (Lawrence 2000, 406).

Congress and the general public (if they were paying attention) believed the revised regulations would help protect women from involuntary sterilizations; however, it did not take long for accusations to surface that IHS was still sterilizing women without their informed consent and was not following HEW regulations. Native American doctors and hospital personnel from Oklahoma and New Mexico sent letters to Senator James Abourezk of South Dakota, chairman of the Senate Interior Subcommittee on Indian Affairs about sterilization abuses (Lawrence 2000, 406).

Gary Rutecki, MD (2010), writes that centuries ago, the British suggested that the response to the presence of Native Americans should be extermination (Patterson and Runge cited in Rutecki 2010). To stress the point of physician cooperation with national eugenics policies, Rutecki suggests that sterilization may have been a partial solution to achieve these ends. Rutecki points to allegations of failing to provide women with necessary information as required in the HEW regulations. Because of a steep decline in birth rates in the Native American population, the Government Accounting Office (GAO) launched an investigation. In 1976, the GAO investigated four of twelve Indian Health Service hospitals in Albuquerque, Aberdeen, Oklahoma City, and Phoenix (Rutecki 2010, n.p.). Investigators found that IHS performed 3,406 sterilizations from 1973 to 1976 (Larson 1977). Looking back at the population per capita, this figure would be equivalent to sterilizing 452,000 non-Native women (Wagner 1977). As Rutecki (2010, n.p.) points out, "Albuquerque contracted out their sterilizations to local, non-IHS physicians; therefore their region inaccurately added zero procedures to the government count. . . . Independent verifications were critical, but the GAO did not interview a single woman subjected to sterilization." Rutecki (2010, n.p.) writes that the GAO "admitted that contract physicians were not required to comply with any federal regulations (including informed consent) in the context of these surgical procedures, and study of consent forms revealed 'consent,' in many cases, was obtained through coercion." This means that none of the four service areas studied were in compliance with government regulations regarding informed consent.

The GAO found two deficiencies in the sterilization practices of the Indian Health Service. First, the IHS area offices failed to follow HEW regulations pertaining to sterilizations. Second, IHS headquarters did not provide specific directions to the area offices for the new regulations and did not provide guidelines for the area offices to use in implementing the procedures. Deficiencies were attributed to HEW's "inability to develop specific sterilization guidelines and a standardized consent form for all its agencies to use" (Comptroller of the United States 1976, 25, 26).

Even worse is that physicians and health care professionals in IHS coerced these women, thereby disregarding their professional responsibility to protect these vulnerable women by ignoring appropriate and informed consent prior to the procedures. On the Navajo Nation, from 1972 to 1978, sterilization procedures went from 15.1 percent to 30.7 percent of total female surgeries on this reservation alone (Temkin-Greener, Kunitz, Broudy, and Haffner 1981). During this period, Native women living on reservations were coerced by health care professionals telling them that future health care would be withdrawn or their children—already born—could be taken from them if consent for sterilization was withheld (Torpy 2000).

Native Americans were outraged and accused IHS of making genocide part of its policy. IHS officials responded that the word *genocide* was unwarranted and the GAO report did not prove forced sterilization, that consent documents were on file, and that it was not possible to tell whether Indians were being sterilized at a higher rate than other women in the general population (Larson 1977). This is nothing less than a replay of earlier twentieth-century eugenic programs and genocidal tactics that led to the congressional hearing, but nevertheless, very little publicity, justice, or public outcry followed (Rutecki 2010).

Once the word spread through Indian Country that young women were still being coerced into sterilization, some tribal leaders carried out their own investigation. On the Northern Cheyenne Reservation, a tribal judge interviewed fifty women and found that twenty-six had been sterilized. Some women were told they had several children and it was time to stop having more. Other women were told they could have children after the operation. Doctors failed to recognize that the values American Indians hold toward the number of children they can bear are much different than those of white America (Dillingham 1977). Accusing IHS of genocidal practices was a very serious accusation, and it was not far off base. In his book on the politics of population control, Littlewood (1977, 82) writes, "Non-white Americans are not unaware of how the American Indian came to be called the vanishing American . . . this country's starkest example of genocide in practice."

One thing is clear: IHS damaged tribal communities by eliminating much of their ability to reproduce, as well as respect for them as tribal entities, and the political power of their tribal councils. The level of power of a community's tribal government is affected by the number of people in that community. Therefore, a lowered census number may have a negative effect on federal services a tribal community receives. And, importantly, a tribal community that suffers a great loss in numbers due to sterilizations can lose the respect of other tribal communities because of its inability to protect its women (Lynch 1981). In addition, Native American women seldom reveal their thoughts on family planning or sterilization. One author conducted several interviews revealing ways in which these women believe the procedure directly affected their lives. The following is one story:

> Employees from a nearby IHS hospital approached Janet about sterilization in 1973. Janet was 29 and had three children. The social workers came to her house six times when her husband was at work. "They told me that I should be sterilized because I didn't want any more babies right then, so I said yes and signed a consent form. My tubes were tied the next day." Janet found out that the sterilization was irreversible during an American Indian Movement demonstration against IHS sterilizations at Claremore, Oklahoma, in 1974. For the next fifteen years a psychiatrist treated Janet for severe depression. Her youngest daughter still refuses to use IHS for any type of medical care. (Lawrence 2000, 413)

CONCLUSION

Native Americans have survived through colonization, termination, assimilation, and genocidal practices. Children are the future of tribal nations, and Native American women who experienced coerced and involuntary sterilization will forever be scarred physically, emotionally, mentally, and spiritually. Indigenous people and tribal nations continue to struggle to have their voices heard and to be recognized as having equal human rights, self-determination, and sovereignty. Forced and coerced sterilization will always be part of their past. The brutal U.S. sterilization policies to control undesirable populations left behind thousands of broken young women who would have to face the fact they might never be able to have children of their own. Broken trust, debilitating medical side effects, depression, and other psychological conditions grew from the seeds of eugenics and government policies with destructive consequences.

Although great harm occurred in the 1960s and 1970s, American Indian participation in their own health care since 1976 has strengthened tribal communities. Lawrence (2000, 415) states *"that does not mean steriliza-tion cannot happen again"* (author's emphasis). The Department of Health, Education, and Welfare does not audit IHS programs; it only audits the computer records on reported sterilizations, and until HEW conducts full audits on all sterilizations that the federal government funds, sterilization abuse will continue to be a cause of concern for Native Americans.

The appallingly enormous and unknown number of sterilizations that diminished Indigenous populations left a political and economic void and silenced voices in tribes and communities that cannot be replaced. The extent of violence and eradication brought about by colonization practices of superiority has been disturbingly concealed and provides historical context to what could happen in the future. The importance of revisiting sterilization of Indigenous peoples and learning the history of this trag-edy may help ensure that future generations of marginalized peoples may never have to face such atrocities again.

REFERENCES

Arsenault, Chris. 2015. "Coerced Sterilization of Canadian Indigenous Women in 70s Widespread." Reuters. http://www.reuters.com/article/us-canada-women -health/coerced-sterilization-of-canadian-indigenous-women-in-70s -widespread-researcher-idUSKCN0R12QM20150901.

Churchill, Ward. 1997. *A Little Matter of Genocide: Holocaust and Denial in the Americas 1492 to the Present*. San Francisco: City Lights Books.

Comptroller of the United States. 1976. *Investigations of Allegations Concerning Indian Health Services*. Washington, D.C.: Government Printing Office.

Dillingham, Brint. 1977. "Indian Women and IHS Sterilization Practices." *American Indian Journal of the Institute for the Development of Indian Law* 3 (1): 27–28.

Echo-Hawk, Walter R. 2010. *In the Courts of the Conqueror: The 10 Worst Indian Law Cases Ever Decided*. Golden, CO: Fulcrum.

Hall, Kermit L. 1992. *The Oxford Companion to the Supreme Court of the United States*. New York: Oxford University Press.

Hiller, Marc D. 1981. *Medical Ethics and the Law: Implications for Public Policy*. Cambridge, MA: Ballinger.

Jabour, Bridie. 2015. "UN Examines Australia's Forced Sterilization of Women with Disabilities." *The Guardian*, November 10. https://www.theguardian.com /australia-news/2015/nov/10/un-examines-australias-forced-sterilisation-of -women-with-disabilities.

Krase, Kathryn. 2014. *History of Forced Sterilization and Current U.S. Abuses*. www .ourbodiesourselves.org/health-info/forced-sterilization.

Larson, K. 1977. "And Then There Were None." *Christian Century* (January): 61, 63.

Laughlin, Harry H. 1926. *Historical, Legal, and Statistical Review of Eugenical Sterilization in the United States*. New Haven, CT: American Eugenics Society.

Lawrence, Jane. 2000. "The Indian Health Service and the Sterilization of Native American Women." *American Indian Quarterly* 24 (3): 400–19.

Littlewood, Thomas B. 1977. *The Politics of Population Control*. Notre Dame, IN: University of Notre Dame Press.

Lynch, Rosemary. 1981. "Leadership and Tribal Government." *Bismarck Tribune*, October 23, 49.

Miller, Mark, Judith Miller, and Chris Szechenyl. 1978. "Native American Peoples on the Trail of Tears Once More." *America* 139 (December 9): 423.

Neubeck, Kenneth J., and Noel A. Cazenave. 2001. *Welfare: Playing the Race Card Against America's Poor*. New York: Routledge.

Nicholson, Lucy. 2014. "Confirmed: 39 Women Illegally Sterilized in California Prisons." *Reuters*, June 6. http://www.rt.com/usa/167660-california-illegal -sterilization-women.

Relf, Katie et al., plaintiffs, v. Casper W. Weinberger et al., defendants [and] National Welfare Rights Organization, plaintiff, v. Casper W. Weinberger et al., defendants. 1974. Washington, D.C.: *Federal Supplement: Cases Argued and Determined in the United States District Courts, United States Customs Courts, and Rulings of the Judicial Panel on Multidistrict Litigation*, 372.

Reynolds, H. R. 2005. *Nowhere People*. Camberwell, Victoria, Australia: Penguin.

Rutecki, G. 2010. "Forced Sterilization of Native Americans: Late Twentieth Century Physician Cooperation with National Eugenic Policies" (podcast). The Center for Bioethics & Human Dignity, Trinity International University.

Sloan, Blythe, Beny Weischedel, and Alia Yasen. 2010. *Race, Racism, and Human Genetics* (blog). Willamette University. http://raceandgenetics.blogspot.com /2010/10/sterilization-in-united-states.

Stern, A. M. 2005. "Sterilized in the Name of Public Health: Race, Immigration, and Reproductive Control in Modern California." *American Journal of Public Health* 95: 1128–38.

Temkin-Greener, S., J. Kunitz, D. Broudy, and M. Haffner. 1981. "Surgical Fertility Regulation Among Women on the Navajo Indian Reservation, 1972–1978." *American Journal of Public Health* 71: 403–7.

Torpy, S. J. 2000. "Native American Women and Coerced Sterilization: On the Trail of Tears in the 1970s." *American Indian Culture and Research Journal* 24: 1–22.

Volscho, Thomas W. 2010. "Sterilization Racism and Pan-Ethic Disparities of the Past Decade: The Continued Encroachment on Reproductive Rights." *Wicazo Sa Review* 25 (1): 17–31.

Wade, Lisa. 2011. "Sterilization of Women of Color: Does 'Unforced' Mean 'Freely Chosen'?" https://thesocietypages.org/socimages/2016/07/15/breaking-down -the-forcechoice-binary-in-the-sterilization-of-women-of-color/comment -page-1/#comment-523308.

Wanhalla, Angela. 2007. "'To 'Better the Breed of Men': Women and Eugenics in New Zealand, 1900–1935." *Women's History Review* 16 (2): 163–82.

Wagner, Bill 1977 "To the Poor and Sterilized Indian." *America* 136 (4): 75.

Weisbord, Robert G. 1975. *Genocide? Birth Control and the Black American*. Westport, CT: Greenwood Press.

LEGAL RESOURCES

Scholendorff v. Society of New York 1914, 105 NE 92, 211 N.Y. 125.

Skinner v. Oklahoma 1942, 316 U.S. 535.

3

THE GREAT GAMBLER

Indian Gaming, Crime, and Misconception

CHERYL REDHORSE BENNETT

N 2008, the Indian Gaming Regulatory Act celebrated its twenty-year anniversary. At the Fort McDowell Resort and Casino in Fountain Hills, Arizona, tribal leaders and legislators from across the country came together to examine and reflect on the last two decades of Indian gaming and what it has meant to their respective communities. Throughout the three-day conference, major players in Indian[1] gaming reflected on the tumultuous beginnings of Indian gaming as well as the future of the Indian gaming industry and new challenges ahead. They noted how far they had come in the fight for Indian gaming. Tribes who implement Indian gaming have overcome many challenges and in some cases are still engaged in a constant struggle to exert their tribal sovereignty.

During the last thirty years, Indian gaming has changed the scope and dynamics of Indian Country. Previously impoverished tribes living in third-world conditions, without running water and electricity, struggling to survive, are now major players in politics, government, and economic growth. Indian gaming, now a multibillion dollar industry, has changed the face of Indian Country and the nation as a whole. Tribes previously struggled to survive, living in terrible poverty. Now the tables have turned. Tribes that were once invisible and voiceless are now the driving force in federal Indian policy nationwide (Akee, Spilde, and Taylor 2015).

Tribal leaders have said that the success of Indian gaming has surpassed their wildest dreams. As these tribes have become more successful, they share their wealth with neighboring communities, help tribes in need, and donate to charitable organizations (Akee et al. 2015). This chapter grew out of my reflections after five years' experience living and working as an educational consultant for a very successful gaming tribe in Southern California. Prior to 2003, as a member of the Navajo Nation, I had no knowledge of the scale and dynamics of Indian gaming in California.

Though there are many successful attributes of Indian gaming, opponents have continuously pointed to the negatives, asserting a threat of serious criminal activity. Anti-Indian groups have sprung up just as fast as Indian casinos, claiming that Indian gaming causes crime, deteriorates neighborhoods, and gives Indians special privileges in the form of casinos and sovereignty. The question remains, however: Does Indian gaming bring more crime to reservations and neighboring communities?

INDIAN CASINOS: CESSPOOLS OF CRIMINAL ACTIVITY?

For years, opponents of Indian gaming have claimed ties to organized crime. A new salacious account of Indian gaming negatively portrays gaming and grossly sullies the definition and meaning of tribal sovereignty. Donald Craig Mitchell (2016) outrageously claims that Indian gaming was wholly started by non-Indians with ties to the Italian mafia. His "evidence" is anecdotal at best and, at worst, a dangerously racist viewpoint that characterizes most gaming tribes, and definitely the most successful, as greedy, law-bending criminals. There is not enough evidence to conclude that tribes have had ties to the Italian mafia and to make such a statement negatively portraying the Indian gaming industry.

Gaming in general has a negative perception and portrayal. Las Vegas for example, has the slogan, "What happens in Vegas, stays in Vegas." The city grew as a gambling mecca in the 1930s and banks on its slogan and the promise to provide visitors with a visit full of illicit activity. Gaming has a reputation of preying on the weak and addicted and is rife with stories of people losing their homes and families because of gambling addiction. Indian gaming is even more controversial. Many of those opposed to Indian gaming have argued that Indian gaming causes crime rates in their non-Indian communities to rise, but is that true?

In the early years of Indian gaming, tribes that decided to venture into gaming did so because they had few other options for economic development. Indian gaming met opposition from the beginning from the states. In Florida, the Seminole conducted bingo, and some of the first legal cases involving gaming had to do with the state of Florida attempting to exert control over Seminole gaming. By the 1980s, tribes across the country, but especially in California, had followed the Seminole Nation of Florida's lead. In 1986, the state of California tried to shut down gaming operations on the Morongo and Cabazon reservations. The Indio police raided the Cabazon card gaming operation. A series of court cases followed in California state court that ended in a 1987 decision (*California v. Cabazon Band of Indians*). The Supreme Court upheld the right of tribes to conduct gaming operations. In a majority opinion, the Court argued that tribes fell under the federal government, not the states, because they are "domestic dependent" nations. California argued that they had jurisdiction over gaming operations simply on the basis of being a Public Law 280 state.[2] To that point, the Court also ruled against California, using the public policy test and pointing out that since California had a state-run lottery, gambling—"as a matter of public policy"—was not illegal and that therefore the authority California was attempting to assert was *civil and regulatory*, rather than criminal, jurisdiction. Within the majority opinion, state jurisdiction was rejected under the Organized Crime Control Act, even though California is a Public Law 280 state (Mason 2000).

> We conclude that the State's interest in preventing the infiltration of the tribal bingo enterprises by organized crime does not justify state regulation of the tribal bingo enterprises in light of the compelling federal and tribal interests supporting them. State regulation would permissibly infringe on tribal government, and this conclusion applies equally to the county's attempted regulation of the Cabazon card club. (*California v. Cabazon Band of Indians* 1987)

After the Supreme Court's decision, it became imperative for those opposed to gaming to pressure Congress to pass the Indian Gaming Regulatory Act (Mason 2000). Opponents continued to point to the looming threat of organized crime running rampant on reservations. They sought to halt the expansion of gaming, to essentially rein it in, so that states could have some measure of control over it and be included in the profits. During the initial Senate hearings, opponents brought forth several concerns about gaming, one being the "need to control criminal activity associated with gambling and the alleged inability of tribes to deal with such crime" (Mason 2000, 55).

After many years of hearings, the Indian Gaming Regulatory Act (IGRA) was passed in 1988. Tribes have said that Indian gaming is one of the most regulated industries in the United States. Multiple governments oversee gaming, depending on the gaming classification, including the FBI, states, and the National Indian Gaming Commission, among others. But with all the regulation, there are still allegations of organized crime on reservations. Where do these allegations come from?

According to a 1991 *Los Angeles Times* exposé, the Chicago mafia tried to get a hold in gaming on the Rincon Band of Luiseno reservation in the late 1980s. The *Times* claimed numerous FBI surveillance recordings detailed the extent of the effort by the mafia to try to gain control of gaming at Rincon. Chris Petti, a non-Indian with Chicago mafia ties, tried and failed to gain control of the Rincon casino. Petti and associates attempted to secure a proposal to run the Rincon casino. Rincon's casino struggled for years and shut down several times because it was not making money. In the beginning, Indian gaming was rife with non-Indian proposals to conduct business with tribes. Tribes were constantly approached by non-Indian investors, some of whom only wanted to take advantage of the tribes. Petti's scheme did not work, but the allegations of mafia infiltration continued to plague Indian gaming. Rincon tribal members were skeptical of the mafia claims and consider it "baloney," with little basis in fact (Liberman 1991).

Currently, the Rincon Band of Luiseno is one of the most successful gaming tribes in the state of California and operates a Harrah's Casino Resort. They have diversified their economic development to include businesses other than casinos. They are very successful, and there is no current news of illegal activity. So, again, where do these allegations come from? It appears that the bulk of allegations that Indian casinos are rife with organized crime come from those that would benefit most from sullying the image of Indian gaming. According to Dunstan (1997, n.p.),

Competitors and antigambling interests use that charge as an attack on Indian gaming. Some researchers and industry observers are quick to point out that, however, there is no evidence that organized crime has significantly infiltrated Indian gambling operations. Others counter that inadequate regulation and oversight make it harder to find evidence. But there is ample evidence of attempts, some of which have met with success. . . . There have been other incidents. Two tribal leaders who had complained that Indians weren't getting a fair share of gambling profits at another facility were later murdered. At the Barona Reservation, a bingo manager was caught rigging games so that shills in the audience could win. Later, he testified about mob involvement in a number of Indian casinos throughout the country. Some of what he said has been substantiated. These events did occur, however, during the earlier years of Indian gaming.

These allegations of mafia ties to the Barona reservation are unsubstantiated. In the literature, scholars, researchers, and state legislators agree that the rumors about Indian casinos and mafia connections are blown out of proportion in order to fulfill the agenda of opponents to Indian gaming and anti-Indian groups (Mason 2000). The most recent allegations only draw on anecdotal information (Mitchell 2016).

It is complicated to answer the question posed earlier: Does Indian gaming increase crime on reservations and off reservation? Generally, it does not increase crime. According to Taylor, Krepps, and Wang (2000, 14), the statistics they analyzed did not demonstrate any increase in crime when casinos were introduced. There is no evidence that crime has increased in communities in which there is an Indian casino:

> Trump, as well as state governors and other government officials, was claiming that Indian gaming was out of control, corrupt, and in dire need of stricter governmental regulation. In testimony before a Congressional hearing in October 1993, Trump stated that "it's obvious that organized crime is rampant on the Indian reservations. This thing is going to blow sky high. It will be the biggest scandal since Al Capone, and it will destroy the gaming industry." The FBI refuted these statements and has testified that it has not detected major incursions by organized crime into Indian gaming around the country. (Slack 1994, n.p.)

Admittedly, some tribes who own and operate gaming operations have had criminal activity on their reservations, examples of which are discussed later in this chapter. But whether there is an increase in their criminal activity *because* of gaming can only be speculated upon.

According to Mason (2000), Dan Inouye remarked that the main factor behind the regulation of Indian gaming was economical rather than solely to thwart organized crime. States saw tribes as competition to their gaming enterprises. However, added factors of racism and white privilege must be looked at to understand the unique position of Indian gaming in the United States.

INDIAN GAMING AND INDIAN HATING

Federal Indian policy scholars have explained that the backlash against Indian gaming is in part due to non-Indians not understanding Indian gaming, as well as ignorance about tribal sovereignty (Wilkinson 2005). Though that may be the case, there is an undeniable element of anti-Indianism in the United States. This is evident in other fights for rights and sovereignty, such as in the activism surrounding the Dakota Access Pipeline. Thousands of activists descended upon the Sacred Stone Camp to show solidarity and support for the Lakotas. The media provided only minimal coverage of the protests until the federal government interfered to end the protest, and the vicious attacks by private security who used attack dogs on peaceful water protectors was nearly invisible. Nearby communities did not show much support and heightened the situation by spinning rumors that the water protectors were armed, violent, and dangerous. Graffiti sprayed on walls read "Fuck Indians." Social media was rife with Indian hating. This is just a small example of the types of hate that happen in the Northern Plains and reservation border towns.

Indian gaming has been the target of the same type of anti-Indianism. The wealthiest tribes have dealt with jealousy by lawmakers and neighboring communities (Corntassel 2008). The Mashantucket Pequot have withstood racism regarding their "low blood quantum." Their neighbors have accused them of being a fake tribe and taking advantage of the system. Other newly recognized tribes and those up for federal recognition have dealt with the same types of reactions, that they are "fake Indians" and aiming for recognition only to cash in on casino profits (Mitchell 2016).

Anti-sovereignty groups have protested outside of casinos, arguing that tribal sovereignty in un-American. In addition to anti-Indianism is a new stereotype that all Indians are newly rich with casino wealth, when in reality only a handful of tribes have seen large profits. In some cases the non-Indian community is jealous of the wealth. There is an underlying racist perception that American Indians should not be wealthy. An American Indian student told me once that when they discussed genocide in her history class, the white professor joked, "But everything is okay now, because they have casinos."

OTHER FACTORS BEHIND CRIME RATES

American Indians have the highest rates of violence committed against them of any race or ethnic group. According to recent reports, American Indians are killed by police at a high rate, considering that the overall population of American Indians is 5.4 million, or 2 percent of the population (U.S. Census Bureau 2010; Woodard 2016). American Indians are also incarcerated at a higher rate than other racial and ethnic groups. These facts are the result of a variety of factors related to colonization (Nielsen 2009). The colonization of American Indian people occurred on multiple fronts. They were physically removed from ancestral territories, murdered, assaulted, raped, and then put under federal Indian laws and policies that sought to continue the colonization. Scholars that research crime in Indian Country have asserted that these high rates are directly correlated to lack of jurisdiction and the tangled jurisdictional maze that is tribal criminal law (Deloria and Lytle 1983).

COLONIZATION

Prior to colonization, there were social and cultural mechanisms in place to curb crime and inappropriate behavior among members of the same tribe. Internalized colonization explains the proclivity toward Indian-on-Indian crime today. In many tribal communities murder was forbidden; the punishment was severe. Banishment was not uncommon among certain groups. Peacemaking was the Navajo form of handling disputes. Instructions were given in stories about appropriate ways to treat relatives and fellow tribal members. After colonization, the reservation period, and the boarding school system, these ways of being were eroded, if not completely destroyed.

Some of the wealthiest tribes have the same social and criminal issues on their reservations as some of the poorest communities. They have issues with alcoholism and drug abuse, and even gang activity. There have been claims, for example, that the St. Regis Mohawk tribal members are involved in drug trafficking. "Casino money has also fueled the surge, providing a fast-growing source of customers and well-financed partners for outside drug traffickers" ("Drug Traffickers" 2006, n.p.). The St. Regis Mohawk have denied that the trafficking is widespread and do not like the characterization portraying members of their nation.

MURDER FOR HIRE IN THE DESERT

Historians and scholars of American history often balk at the word *geno-cide*. But most agree that genocide is an appropriate word to describe the atrocities committed against the California Indians. By 1900, the population of California Indians decreased from over 300,000 to less than 16,000 people (Castillo n.d.). Until the early twentieth century, bounties were placed on California Indians so that they were nearly obliterated. The remainder are the survivors of the mission system, gold rush, rape, murder, massacre, and slavery. This is why there is such a small population of California Indians, and there are tribes comprised of two hundred to as few as one person. The genocide in California was nearly successful. In addition, there are unratified treaties. Many of their reservations were hilly with rocky terrain, and on some reservations they literally had to dynamite the hills to make an area flat enough to accommodate housing and later casinos. Several factors have determined the economic wealth of the California casinos: small tribes, location, and proximity to wealth.

GAMING IN SOUTHERN CALIFORNIA

Indian gaming in Southern California is quite different from that on the Navajo Nation. The climate for gaming is also unique. The small tribes, coupled with the location of the casinos and amount of wealth in California, have made Indian gaming in California a billion-dollar industry (Akee et al. 2015; Contreras 2006). The San Manuel Band of Mission Indians is a small tribe located in San Bernardino, California, with a membership of approximately two hundred.

In 2006, members of the San Manuel Band of Mission Indians Stacy Nunez-Barajas and Erik Barajas placed a hit on Leonard Epps, a non-tribal member and non-Indian. Epps, who worked with law enforcement, reportedly faked his death and went into hiding so that the Barajas siblings would believe that the hit had been successful. During this time, the news media ran a series of articles accusing other members of the San Manuel Band of Mission Indians of a variety of crimes including drug possession, drug trafficking, and having ties to the Mexican mafia. The Mexican mafia was also allegedly extorting money from some of the members of the San Manuel Band of Mission Indians. During this time the image of gaming in Southern California became very negative.

As discussed previously, when gaming started in California and Florida, the argument against gaming had been that organized crime would take hold of Indian gaming. The murder-for-hire plot added to the already precarious image of gaming in Southern California. San Manuel had been at the forefront of the Indian gaming movement. In the 1990s they along with other tribes had joined together to pass Proposition 5, fighting for their sovereign rights and the right to game. During the battle to pass Proposition 5, antigaming ads ran showing aerial footage of the small reservation and the "mansions of San Manuel" (Akee et al. 2015; Contreras 2006). San Manuel fought to change the image of gaming and even after Proposition 5 was passed had an aggressive and strategic marketing campaign. Since the passage of Proposition 5, the tribe has created commercials aired on major networks in Southern California that explain what sovereignty is and how non-Indians benefit from gaming, as well as correct common misconceptions such as the belief that American Indians do not pay taxes (Akee et al. 2015; Contreras 2006).

Prior to gaming, tribes in Southern California lived like many of the poorest tribes in the nation. In the documentary *California's Lost Tribes*, the tribal leader from Morongo discussed the conditions on the Morongo Indian reservation. They did not have running water, and very few families lived on the reservation. This was the common lived experience of most of the Indians in Southern California at this time (Riffe 2005).

After the murder-for-hire scandal, Stacy Nunez-Barajas pled guilty to attempted murder, with a gang enhancement increasing her sentence, and drug charges. Initially, Nunez-Barajas was sentenced to electronic monitoring and probation, but she violated the terms of her parole. She is currently serving a seventeen-year prison sentence. Erik Barajas pled guilty to assault with a deadly weapon with a gang enhancement increasing his sentence. He was sentenced to electronic monitoring and probation (Morales 2008).

In 2009, the San Manuel Band of Mission Indians banished both siblings, Nunez-Barajas and Barajas, from the reservation. James Ramos, tribal chairman at the time, said, "I'm not saying that crime is running rampant, but it's a problem" (Kelly 2008, n.p.). The band claimed that they had taken steps to curb criminal activity but did not disclose whether the per capita payments the siblings received were also stopped. Leonard Epps filed a civil suit against the Barajas. Epps claimed that he had to go into hiding and still feared for his life. A jury awarded him $4.5 million in compensatory damages and $2 million in punitive damages (Nelson 2013).

Per capita payments remain a controversial topic within the Indian gaming conversation. The assumption was made in the news that the tribe's per capita payments led to criminal activity; however, it has been discussed in the literature that crime in Indian Country is prevalent primarily due to colonization and lack of jurisdiction. In fact, the positive impact per capita has had on tribal economies has been noted (Conner and Taggart 2013). However, there is a need for more research regarding per capita and its impact on the social fabric of tribal communities.

THE GAMING CONTROVERSY
ON THE NAVAJO NATION

In 2008, Firerock Casino opened near Gallup, New Mexico. As a Diné (Navajo), I had mixed feelings about the project but was hopeful at the prospect of employment opportunities for the Navajo people. The Diné have some of the highest unemployment rates in the country. In some areas on Navajo land, there is no running water or electricity. My family still hauls in water to their homes near Bisti Badlands. However, I also could not help feeling disappointed, being proud that the Navajo Nation and Navajo people had previously stood firm to their morals, culture, and teaching and voted against gaming.

In previous scholarship, I answered the question of whether Indian gaming has a positive or negative impact (Bennett 2010). For the most part, the impact is positive. Gaming has been called the "new buffalo," the catalyst through which tribes can pull themselves out of poverty and buy into the American dream. But can money alone solve the problems that American Indian nations face? As mentioned previously, some very wealthy tribes have the same social, criminal, and spiritual issues that the poorest reservations have. In some instances, instant wealth appears to make the problems more acute.

There is a very old Navajo story from near the Bisti Badlands on the northern periphery of Navajo land. The landscape of Bisti is reminiscent of the moon. Photographers, tourists, and filmmakers have traveled to the Bisti Badlands to capture the white hills and dips and craters in the terrain. It is beautiful. Nearby, several miles south of the Bisti Badlands, is Chaco Canyon. There are many stories from the area, but some of them have been lost. Navajo stories tend to be regional, with specific events marking the difference or variation among the tales. The story of the Great Gambler and the White Butterfly that follows is specific to this area of Navajo land.

In the days of the Anasazi (the ancient ones), there was a great and terrible being that came from the south known as the Great Gambler. He challenged the people to a footrace and other games of chance, and he enslaved them when they lost.

When the wandering Navajos arrived at Kintyeli, this great pueblo was in process of building, but was not finished. The way it came to be built was this—

Some time before, there had descended among the Pueblos, from the heavens, a divine gambler or gambling-god, named Noqoilpi, or He-who-wins-men (at play): his talisman was a great piece of turquoise. When he came, he challenged the people to all sorts of games and contests, and in all of these he was successful. He won from them, first their property, then their women and children, and finally some of the men themselves. Then he told them he would give them part of their property back in payment if they would build a great house; so when the Navajos came, the Pueblos were busy building, in order that they might release their enthralled relatives and their property. They were also busy making a race-track, and preparing for all kinds of games of chance and skill. (Matthews 1889, 89)

The Great Gambler's slaves built Chaco Canyon. In varying accounts, the Great Gambler is always defeated by a hero when he loses at the games of chance presented to him. In some versions, he is not killed but sent south to Mexico to be the god of the people there. Some stories claim that the Great Gambler will return one day. This is the story and warning that is most well-known among the Navajo. There is another story that is lesser known.

Navajo hero Downey Home Man[3] rescues ten girls being held by a man called Earth Winner (Great Gambler). "He beats everyone at gambling and wins girls." The girls were held in a kiva at Wide House, which is the present-day Aztec Ruins. Downey Home Man changes into a butterfly, flies into the kiva, and leads the girls out to safety. Earth Winner is full of trickery and changes into a white butterfly "to lure them away from the young man." Downey Home Man and White Butterfly play a series of games. Downey Home Man enlists the aid of other Navajo deities and proceeds to beat White Butterfly in three games. The fourth game they play is a footrace. "They bet everything, the earth, flowers, and trees and themselves. Downey Home Man wins the race, kills White Butterfly, and returns the ten wives to their homes" (Kelley and Francis 1994, 112).

The Navajo are not antigambling. Many cultural gambling games are played for fun and entertainment, primarily in the wintertime. But these stories serve to warn the people about the excesses of gambling. In each tale, the Great Gambler entices the people to play games to excess. In my observation, the story of the Great Gambler has been a main factor behind the decision of the Navajo people to continuously vote against gaming.

Navajos opened the first casino on the Navajo Nation in November 2008. The Firerock Casino has been successful, with its patrons primarily being Navajo. Within the first three months of its opening there were sixty-three arrests made, "mostly for alcohol related crimes." There were also domestic disputes, and "31 were removed for bringing drugs or alcohol onto the premises" (Donovan 2010, n.p.). By the time Firerock opened its doors, the market was already saturated with casinos and Firerock was just one of many tribal casinos along Interstate 40. There are now four casinos on the reservation. In 2015, the four casinos brought in nearly $120 million (Palermo 2016), but they still are not as economically successful as the casinos in California or Arizona.

Twin Arrows is the Navajo Nation's first resort-style casino, located east of Flagstaff, Arizona. Within the first few months of its opening in 2013, calls to the Coconino County Sheriff's Office were coming in. The agreement between the county and the tribe is still under negotiation, but two Navajo police officers are scheduled to remain on-site at the casino.

The impact gaming will have on the Navajo Nation and Navajo people is still uncertain. Gaming revenue has funded tribal projects and provided jobs for tribal members but has also negatively impacted some Navajo families who have gambling addictions. But like the examples provided, some of these social issues predate gaming. Gambling addiction may have been present before the Navajo casinos. Because of population size, the Navajo Nation will never see the type of gaming wealth that tribes in California, Minnesota, and New England have obtained.

CONCLUSION

Yes, in some cases Indian gaming has demonstrated that tribes can support themselves, exercise sovereignty, and revitalize language, cultures, and economies. The dark side of Indian gaming has shown another human story. Indian Country is inundated with stories of disenrollment, per capita payments, and greed (Fenelon 2006). In some instances, tribal members have been unprepared for immense wealth and the social and spiritual toll capitalism would take on their people. Taiaiake Alfred (2005, 211–12), Indigenous warrior scholar, explores the questions "Is there a spiritual and cultural cost of doing business this way? What have the so-called 'gaming tribes' had to sacrifice of their authentic selves in order to gain the political and economic power they now possess? Have they remained true to basic indigenous values and principles in their quest for freedom and power?" These are the more important questions to ask, instead of whether crime increases because of gaming.

These questions must be answered on a case-by-case, tribe-by-tribe basis. There are numerous examples of tribes that use gaming profits to better their nations. Then there are a handful of tribes who have

mismanaged their casinos, been taken advantage of by outsiders, or suc-
cumbed to criminal influences. But the freedom that comes from economic success is undeniable. Alfred (2005, 222) asserts that "we need to
both possess economic power and cultural authenticity."

When analyzing the high propensity for crime on reservations, the
answers to curbing those numbers have to do with jurisdiction and a return
to traditional teachings and values. Even though some tribes may have
criminal activity linked to gaming, this negative does not overshadow the
successes and positive aspects of Indian gaming. Indian gaming has given
tribes the chance to pull their communities out of poverty and revitalize
their cultures. It has been a game changer for American Indian nations
and American Indian people. Indian nations who participate in gaming
have helped other tribal nations in need, created scholarships, given money
to help victims of the bombing at the World Trade Center (Ambler 2001),
and given aid to countless non-Native charities and universities. Critics
always are the first to point to the excesses and potential for crime and to
give examples of criminal activity; however, every tribe must be free and
empowered to be able to determine the course of their nation.

Maori leader Graham Smith (2008) has said that in order for Indigenous nations to be sovereign, they need to act sovereign. Whether we
agree with or support Indian gaming is not the issue because the choice
should not be left to outsiders. It is up to each tribal nation and its people
to determine the course of their own nations.

NOTES

1. The terms *American Indian* and *Indian* are used in this chapter because the
   legal terminology refers to tribes as "American Indian."
2. For an explanation of Public Law 280 (PL-280) please see the introduction
   to part III.
3. He made his bed of bird feathers and that is how he got the name Downey
   Home Man.

REFERENCES

Akee, Randall K. Q., Katherine A. Spilde, and Jonathan B. Taylor. 2015. "The
    Indian Gaming Regulatory Act and Its Effects on American Indian Economic
    Development." *Journal of Economic Perspectives* 29 (3): 185–208.
Alfred, Taiaiake. 2005. *Wasase*. New York: Broadview Press.

Ambler, Marjane. 2001. "We Are All Related." *Tribal College Journal.* http://tribal collegejournal.org/related.

Bennett, Cheryl R. 2010. "The Gambler: The Consequences of Gaming in Southern California." In *The American Mosaic: The American Indian Experience.* http://americanindian.abc-clio.com.

Castillo, Edward. n.d. "A Short Overview of California Indian History." http://www.nativeamericancaucus.org/content/california-indian-history.

Conner, Thaddieus W., and William A. Taggart. 2013. "Assessing the Impact of Indian Gaming on American Indian Nations: Is the House Winning?" *Social Science Quarterly* 94 (5): 1016–44.

Contreras, Kate Spilde. 2006. "Cultivating New Opportunities: Tribal Government Gaming on the Pechanga Reservation." *American Behavioral Scientist* 50: 315–52.

Corntassel, Jeff. 2008. *Forced Federalism: Contemporary Challenges to Indigenous Nationhood.* Norman: University of Oklahoma Press.

Deloria, Vine, Jr., and Clifford Lytle. 1983. *American Indians, American Justice.* Austin: University of Texas Press.

Donovan, Bill. 2010. "Firerock Reports 1,426 Winners Per Month." *Navajo Times.* http://navajotimes.com/business/2010/1210/120210firerock.php.

"Drug Traffickers Find Haven in Shadows of Indian Country." 2006. *New York Times,* February 19. http://www.nytimes.com/2006/02/19/us/drug-traffickers-find-haven-in-shadows-of-indian-country.html?_r=0.

Dunstan, Roger. 1997. "Gambling and Crime." *Gambling in California.* California Research Bureau, California State Library. https://www.library.ca.gov/crb/97/03/crb97003.html.

Fenelon, James V. 2006. "Indian Gaming: Traditional Perspectives and Cultural Sovereignty." *American Behavioral Scientist* 50 (3): 381–409.

Kelley, Klara, and Harris Francis. 1994. *Navajo Sacred Places.* Bloomington: Indiana University Press.

Kelly, David. 2008. "San Manuel Tribe Teams Up with Deputies." *Los Angeles Times,* June 23. http://articles.latimes.com/2008/jun/23/local/me-sanmanuel23.

Liberman, Paul. 1991. "How the Mafia Targeted Tribe's Gambling Business Crime: The Mob Dropped Bid to Infiltrate Games Near San Diego, but Wiretaps Suggest Ties to Other Reservations." *Los Angeles Times,* October 7. http://articles.latimes.com/1991-10-07/news/mn-74_1_san-diego.

Mason, W. Dale. 2000. *Indian Gaming: Tribal Sovereignty and American Politics.* Norman: University of Oklahoma Press.

Matthews, Washington. 1889. "Noqoìlpi, the Gambler: A Navajo Myth." *Journal of American Folklore* 2 (4): 89–94.

Mitchell, Donald Craig. 2016. *Wampum: How Indian Tribes, the Mafia, and an Inattentive Congress Invented Indian Gaming and Created a $28 Billion Gambling Empire*. New York: Overlook Press.

Morales, Victor. 2008. "Tribal Members Get Probation in Highly Publicized Case." Indian Country Today Media Network. https://indiancountrymedia network.com/news/tribal-members-get-probation-in-highly-publicized-case.

Nelson, Joe. 2013. "San Bernardino Man Marked for Death by San Manuel Tribal Members." *San Bernardino Sun*, August 1. http://www.sbsun.com /general-news/20130801/san-bernardino-man-marked-for-death-by-san -manuel-tribal-members-to-get-45-million.

Nielsen, Marianne O. 2009. "Introduction to the Context of Native American Criminal Justice Involvement." In *Criminal Justice in Native America*, eds. Marianne O. Nielsen and Robert A. Silverman, 1–17. Tucson: University of Arizona Press.

Palermo, Dave. 2016. "Better Late Than Never." *Global Gaming Business Magazine*, January 22. http://ggbmagazine.com/article/better-late-than-never.

Riffe, Jed. 2005. *California's Lost Tribes* [DVD]. Los Angeles: Sony.

Slack, Keith. 1994. "Sovereignty and Indian Gaming in the United States." *Cultural Survival Quarterly*, June. https://www.culturalsurvival.org/ourpublications /csq/article/sovereignty-and-indian-gaming-united-states.

Smith, Graham. 2008. "Cultural Well-Being a Tribally Based Indigenous Response." Lecture, Whare Wananga o Awanuiarangi, Indigenous University, Aotearoa, NZ, September.

Taylor, Jonathan, Mathew Krepps, and Patrick Wang. 2000. "The National Evidence on the Socioeconomic Impacts of American Indian Gaming on Non-Indian Communities." https://www.innovations.harvard.edu/sites/default /files/Taylor%20Kreps%202000.pdf.

U.S. Census Bureau. 2010. "The American Indian and Alaska Native Population: 2010." U.S. Department of Commerce, Economics and Statistics Administration. http://www.census.gov/prod/cen2010/briefs/c2010br-10.pdf.

Wilkinson, Charles. 2005. *Blood Struggle*. New York: W. W. Norton.

Woodard, Stephanie. 2016. "The Police Killings No One Is Talking About." *In These Times*, October 17. http://inthesetimes.com/features/native_american _police_killings_native_lives_matter.html.

LEGAL RESOURCES

California v. Cabazon Band of Indians 480 U.S. 202 (1987).

Indian Gaming Regulatory Act PL 100-497 (1988).

PART II

SOCIAL JUSTICE

INTRODUCTION BY MARIANNE O. NIELSEN AND KAREN JARRATT-SNIDER

Human rights are integral to any discussion of social justice for Indigenous people and peoples and have been contravened repeatedly in both historical and more modern times. Acts that would not have been tolerated against individuals and communities of white European descent were perpetrated repeatedly against Indigenous individuals, perhaps because during the colonial era, the belief was that Indigenous peoples were not really people at all or, at best, some inferior version of people. See, for example, Williams's (1990, 74–103) recounting of Spanish colonizing legal theory for examples of this perception. Today, many of the stereotypes promulgated to justify colonial exploitation and mistreatment of Indigenous peoples are still around, but they are now called racism. Their purpose is the same though: to justify the greed to obtain Indigenous resources, and the violence and disrespect shown toward Indigenous individuals. They also legitimize the disinterest and disregard paid toward Indigenous peoples by some lawmakers, decision makers, criminal justice personnel, and the general public (see, for example, Razack 2015).

Many United Nations conventions are relevant to the history of Indigenous peoples in that they illustrate the crimes both legalistic and as defined by social harm theory that were freely committed against Indigenous people and peoples because most of the conventions did not exist at the time. These include Convention on the Prevention and Punishment of the Crime of Genocide (1948), Convention Against Torture and Other Cruel, Inhuman or Degrading Treatment or Punishment (1987), and Convention on the Rights of the Child (1990).

This continuing abuse of Indigenous peoples is one of the reasons for the UN's (2007) Declaration on the Rights of Indigenous Peoples, an important reference point for Indigenous peoples worldwide. Unfortunately, although this convention has been signed by most countries in the world, many countries still ignore its contents. Australia, Canada, New Zealand, and the United States, longtime holdouts, are among the most recent signers of the declaration. The declaration has three articles of particular relevance to the human rights discussed in this book: Article 7: The right to life, liberty, and security, so that Indigenous peoples have the right to live freely, be secure and safe, and not be exposed to violence; Article 8: Assimilation or destruction of a culture, so that Indigenous peoples have the right not to be forced to adopt someone else's way of life and culture, and their culture has the right to exist; and Article 9: Belonging to an Indigenous community or nation, so that Indigenous peoples may not be discriminated against because of their Indigenous status (UNICEF 2013).

The two authors in this section approach the issue of social justice and human rights from two directions. First, Ali-Joseph explores resilience and the defiance of human rights violations in sports, as a means of resisting attempted assimilation and discrimination through stereotypes. Second, as Archambeault argues, the interpretation and misuse of legal terminology has been used to deny, diminish, and confuse the rights of Indigenous peoples. Social justice has many more dimensions than are commonly taught, as these authors show us.

REFERENCES

Razack, Sherene. 2015. *Dying from Improvement: Inquests and Inquiries into Indigenous Deaths in Custody.* Toronto, ON: University of
Toronto Press.

United Nations (UN). 1948. Convention on the Prevention and Punishment of the Crime of Genocide. http://www.hrweb.org/legal
/genocide.html.

United Nations (UN). 1987. Convention Against Torture and Other
Cruel, Inhuman or Degrading Treatment or Punishment. http://
www.ohchr.org/EN/ProfessionalInterest/Pages/CAT.aspx.

United Nations (UN). 1990. Convention on the Rights of the Child.
http://www.ohchr.org/EN/ProfessionalInterest/Pages/CRC.aspx.

United Nations (UN). 2007. Declaration on the Rights of Indigenous
Peoples. http://www.tjsl.edu/slomansonb/10.3_Indigenous.pdf.

United Nations Children's Fund (UNICEF). 2013. *Know Your Rights!
United Nations Declaration on the Rights of Indigenous Peoples for
Indigenous Adolescents.* http://files.unicef.org/policyanalysis/rights
/files/HRBAP_UN_Rights_Indig_Peoples.pdf.

Williams, Robert A., Jr. 1990. *The American Indian in Western Legal
Thought: The Discourses of Conquest.* New York: Oxford University
Press.

4

TO BE NATIVE AMERICAN AND NOT AMERICAN INDIAN

An Issue of Indigenous Identity or Historically Blind Politically Correct Labeling?

WILLIAM G. ARCHAMBEAULT

THIS CHAPTER FOCUSES on the justice issues relating to the legal statuses and labels applied to descendants of North America's Indigenous peoples living in the continental United States of America. The term *Indigenous peoples* has different meanings.[1] First, it is used as a general label for today's descendants of the original peoples who inhabited what is now the United States, regardless of legal status. Second, it is an official legal status recognized by the United Nations (n.d.). In 2016–2017, the "water protectors" and international Indigenous movements dominated the popular media over the Dakota Access Pipeline conflict near the Standing Rock Sioux Reservation in North Dakota (see Elbein 2017; Women's Earth 2016; Zambelich and Alexandra 2016), illustrating that *Indigenous* is also a term misused by popular media, politicians, academics, and others as a substitute for *American Indian*, although the most often misused substitution is *Native American*. Such legal misuse of the terms sometimes adds layers of confusion to accurate analyses of situations and discussions of facts.

In the United States, the Constitution allows for federal recognition of only one legal status—American Indian. The Constitution allows the U.S. government to directly negotiate only with one legal Indigenous status—federally recognized Indian nations—concerning the protection of rights, privileges, and governmental financial support. In 1999, the U.S. Supreme Court extended the legal status of American Indian to include Alaskan Village Natives, so the complete designation is American

Indian/Alaska Native. In legal discussions, American Indian is inclusive of Alaska Natives when referring to individuals. When referring to federally recognized governmental entities of these peoples, the term is usually *American Indian tribes* (although some presidential executive orders use the term *Native American*), or for Alaska, *the Native Village of*— is the correct term.

Since the 1960s, political and legislative efforts have attempted to change *American Indian* to *Native American* and mostly failed. During the late 1990s, multiple failed political and legislative efforts attempted to equate Native American with American Indian and to extend the rights, privileges, and governmental financial support due American Indians to other "Native" and non–American Indian groups. Court decisions and government policy seemed to clarify this issue (*Rice v. Cayetano* 2000), but continuing failed efforts were repeated until the second decade of the twenty-first century. Neither the term *Native American* nor the term *Indigenous people* has equivalent legal status in the United States with *American Indian*, referred to as Indian tribes under Article I, Section 8, of the U.S. Constitution (U.S. Department of the Interior n.d.). That said, Indigenous peoples recognized under Canadian law, for example, are entitled to green cards. In the United States no other form of federal rights or support is provided (Smith 2012).

This chapter revolves around three questions. First, is the continued use of the term *Native American* a matter of Indigenous identity or historically blind political correctness? Second, has the overuse of the term obscured academic and political focus on real American Indian issues? Finally, can the same be said in the growing use of the term *Indigenous people*?

U.S. AND CANADIAN CONSTITUTIONS: A COMPARISON OF SUBSTANTIVE LAWS AND CULTURES

During the twentieth and early twenty-first centuries, whenever legal reforms were proposed that impacted American Indigenous peoples or governance of American Indians, Canadian law was often emulated. Some understanding of the U.S. and Canadian constitutions is needed to evaluate the utility of these reforms. To begin with, the United States gained its independence through war with Great Britain according to the terms of the 1783 Treaty of Paris, whereas Canada remained under British rule until 1982 when the Canadian Constitution was enacted. Even now, Canada remains part of the British Commonwealth and may be influenced by its policies.

British influence on Canadian constitutional law governing relations with Indigenous populations arguably began with King George's Royal Proclamation of 1763, examined later, that recognized Indians as having original title to their lands (called Aboriginal title in Canada). By contrast and noted previously, the U.S. Constitution does not. Article 2, Section 2, of the U.S. Constitution gives Congress the authority to make treaties, including with the Indian nations within its borders, but the Constitution neither recognizes nor excludes the recognition of original title by Indian nations, even though the United States agreed to do so in signing the 1783 Treaty of Paris. Instead, it left the issue open to negotiators to apply the principle on a tribe-by-tribe basis until the 1823 decision in *Johnson v. M'Intosh*, essentially ruling that Indians did not have original title and that non-Indians could buy tribal land.

Canadian constitutional law recognizes a broad range of Indigenous peoples, including Treaty Indians, Métis, First Nations, Aboriginal peoples, Inuit, Eskimo, Aleut, and Tlingit, among others. By contrast, U.S. constitutional and governmental policy recognizes only one Indigenous status, the American Indian. Further, since 1824 the authority for recognizing, rejecting, or reclassifying groups, communities, and individuals as American Indian lies with the Bureau of Indian Affairs (BIA), which is part of the U.S. Department of the Interior (n.d.). In other words, the only group of Indigenous people in the United States recognized by the federal government are those who meet the BIA criteria for being an American Indian/Alaska Native and member in good standing of a BIA-recognized Indian nation (tribe) or Alaska Native village. No other Indigenous community or persons are entitled to the legal status, rights, protections, and U.S. governmental support as determined by court decisions and governmental policies of the early twenty-first century and discussed later.

Interestingly, both U.S. and Canada law apply a similar test in determining whether an Indigenous group is entitled to government recognition and support. Both require that applicants meet the standard of Indian, as defined in their respective body of law. As noted, in the United States, the BIA set the standards for federal recognition of Indian (U.S. Department of the Interior n.d.). Similarly, in 2016 the Canadian Supreme Court decision in *Daniels v. Canada* held that the groups of mixed blood and nontribal Indigenous peoples satisfied the Indian test as it applied to Métis and were entitled to government support. Unfortunately, no such status exists for Indigenous people in the United States who do not meet BIA standards for Indian. As discussed later, Indigenous peoples from the United States are either federally recognized (also called BIA certified in this chapter) American Indians or non–federally recognized (non–BIA certified). Even visiting Indian peoples from and recognized by other counties are not entitled to the status of BIA American Indians. Since the word *Indian* plays such a critical role in both U.S. and Canadian constitutional law, where does the term originate?

ORIGINS AND INTERNATIONAL INFLUENCE OF A WORD: *INDIAN*

No one seems to agree on the exact source of the word *Indian* (Online Etymology Dictionary n.d.; The Straight Dope 2001). There is more agreement that *Indian* came from the maps of the European colonial powers from the fifteenth century forward, which designated areas controlled by or inhabited by Indigenous peoples in the Americas. The word is translated into several languages. On British maps the word *Indian* was used; on Portuguese maps *Indios*; on Spanish maps *Indio* or *Indios*; and on French maps *Indien*, *Autones*, or *Autochtones*.

There is also no consensus as to where Columbus intended to sail in 1492, other than west. Since a Portuguese expedition sailed east and founded Portuguese India in 1498, it follows that Columbus may have attempted to find India by sailing west. But the India that he was looking for remains a source of controversy since old European maps labeled most of Southeast Asia as India; other maps referred only to the Indus River Valley in current-day India; still others to islands called the West Indies. Regardless, it follows that the Indigenous people he found might be called Indians. Another explanation is that the term came from letters he wrote to Queen Isabella of Spain, who provided funds for his expedition. Supposedly, Columbus referred to the Indigenous people whom he encountered as "le gente in Dios" (people of God) and "las ninos in Dios" (children of God). Any of these explanations are plausible; none are conclusive.

Although the exact origin of the term *Indian* is hidden in the obscurity of history, its international use in map making is well documented. As colonial world powers from the fifteenth through eighteenth centuries fought over, traded, stole, or managed huge geographical areas in the Americas, maps were created that defined legal and sovereign boundaries for these powers. Maps with supporting documents and measurements were the foundations for colonial and later constitutional law making in the New World. By the eighteenth century, four main colonial powers divided up what is now North America: France, England, Spain, and Russia. At the end of the French and Indian War (also called the Seven Years' War), the French yielded control of the area known today as Canada to England by the terms of the Treaty of Paris (1763), while retaining a huge land mass running the interior of the current United States; this land was later purchased in 1803, known as the Louisiana Purchase. Ignoring Russia's Alaska, by 1764 the British government became the most powerful landholder in North America. Great Britain dominated the fur trade and all other forms of legal commerce in North America until the American Revolution of 1775–1783 (Nies 1996).

When the American Revolution concluded, the new republic consisted only of the original thirteen British colonies along the eastern Atlantic seaboard up to Canada but excluded the British colonies of East and West Florida (today, parts of southern Georgia, Florida, Alabama, Mississippi, and Louisiana) that remained loyal to Great Britain. British map claims included Canada, the East and West Florida Colonies, and lands west of the Mississippi River, giving Britain control of waterways feeding into the Mississippi River to the Gulf of Mexico. In 1803, Jefferson bought the remaining French lands under terms of the Louisiana Purchase. By 1848, the United States had defeated Mexico, seizing all lands north of the Rio Grande, and by 1854, all of California was brought into the union. By 1867, the United States had purchased Alaska from Russia and all the lower forty-eight state and territorial areas were under U.S. control (Nies 1996).

Important from this history is that in all these transactions, maps were used to define the boundaries and borders of the United States. Maps and mapmakers used the word *Indian* and its various language spellings to designate relevant Indian territorial areas. So, in a real sense, mapmakers created the legal statuses and terms *Indian* and *Indian nations*. These were included in later U.S. maps, and the use of these mapmaker terms contributed significantly to the American Revolution because of the way they were applied in the 1763 proclamation by King George III of England.

ROYAL PROCLAMATION OF 1763 AND ITS INFLUENCE ON THE AMERICAN REVOLUTION

It is traditional in academic and popular American Indian literature to view all forms of colonization negatively. However, the Royal Proclamation of 1763 might be considered an exception. It accorded a range of protections for North American Indians under British rule that had profound and lasting effects on the United States. Its provisions also laid the foundation for Canadian law and policy as it exists today. The proclamation was intended to honor agreements made with Indian nations that supported the British cause in the French and Indian War, ending in the 1763 Treaty of Paris. It also gave the colonial office of the British government much greater centralized control over the future of the British colonies in the Americas. The reasons for American colonists to rise against the British were many. Under the proclamation, only the British colonial government could buy land from the Indians and then decide who would be allowed to buy it or what could be done with it. It forbade any settlement or commerce beyond the Allegheny Mountains. It prohibited trapping or trading with the Indians, or engaging in any other economic enterprise, except with a British colonial license to do so. Any violation of these provisions was made a crime against the Crown. The law helped turn loyal Englishmen colonists into American revolutionaries (Nies 1996).

One keystone element of the 1763 proclamation, found today in the Canadian Constitution of 1982, was intentionally omitted from the U.S. Constitution (as well as from the Bill of Rights). This is the presumption that Indians (Aboriginal or Indigenous peoples) hold the original title to all North American lands. Instead, U.S. government treaty negotiators were given the discretion of recognizing this assumption on a tribe-by-tribe treaty basis. This was affirmed in the 1823 U.S. Supreme Court decision *Johnson v. M'Intosh*, in which the Court ruled that Indian nations did not have transferrable original title and that non-Indians could buy Indian lands with the permission of the sovereign United States of America.

THE 1783 TREATY OF PARIS
AND THE 1763 ROYAL PROCLAMATION

The French and other European powers (Corwin 1915) had vested economic and political interests in bringing the American conflict with Great Britain to an end and brokered what would eventually be called the 1783 Treaty of Paris. After long negotiations, compromise language resolved most obstacles to an agreement between Britain and its American colonies, except for British demands that key provisions of the Royal Proclamation of 1763 be written into the treaty. Britain demanded that the United States agree to uphold major provisions of the Royal Proclamation that preserved Indian lands for the Indians by prohibiting settlement, trade, land purchase, or other economic interests beyond the Allegheny Mountains. Additionally, the Americans were expected to recognize that Indians had the original title to all North American lands. The American negotiators—John Adams, Benjamin Franklin, and John Jay—flatly refused to sign the document initially. After all, the Americans had just defeated the British military. The Americans, supported by other European and British economic interests, were determined to open settlement, trade, and economic expansion west of the Allegheny Mountains (National History Day n.d.; Nies 1996).

Though British negotiators were more flexible and pragmatic, King George III had to approve the treaty with the Americans and would not do so unless the provisions of the Royal Proclamation were agreed to in the final treaty. King George, also known as the Mad King, was obsessed with protecting his "Indian children." As a boy in 1730 he met with Cherokee chiefs who had come to petition his father, George II, for protection and developed a special relationship with one of the Cherokee leaders, Attakullakulla (Little Carpenter), according to documents at the Museum of the Cherokee (see Norton n.d.). The king's intractable position may have come from reasoning that although his colonials had defeated his troops on the battlefield, he would not forfeit his honor by breaking his word to the Cherokee, whatever the cost.

History does record that the American delegation eventually signed the 1783 Treaty of Paris, which included some of the 1763 proclamation conditions. It may be speculated that the Americans were given assurances from British and other European negotiators that there would be no negative repercussions from violating them because that is exactly what the United States did, and little notice was taken of these violations. Economic interests in the United States, Britain, France, Holland, and other European countries had too much to gain from not sanctioning U.S. treaty violations.

The 1783 Treaty of Paris included both detailed and general maps as well as supporting legal title documents, granting the United States recognition as an independent nation. In turn, words such as *Indian*, *Indian nations*, and *Indian territory* were incorporated into the U.S. Constitution, maps, and other documents (U.S. Department of State n.d.). Congress was given the authority to make treaties with the "Indian nations" within its borders, but the Constitution failed to recognize that Indians had original title. In many ways, the signing of the 1783 Treaty of Paris established the U.S. government precedent in later treaty negotiations with American Indians, characterized often as being deceptive and inconsistent and reflecting little concern about Indian rights or welfare.

THE UNITED STATES CONSTITUTION OF 1788 AND THE POWER OF THE BIA

The wording of the U.S. Constitution was shaped by colonial ideological values and attitudes toward Indians in 1788. It was a document written by people who had experienced the horrors of periodic Indian raids both prior to and during the French and Indian War (1754–1763) and Indian warfare in the American War of Independence (1775–1783). American interests, property, and lives had been taken in warfare by powerful Indian tribes and confederations, including the Mohawk, Cherokee, Shawnee, and tribes of the Haudenosaunee Confederation, among others. During the American Revolution, some tribes favored the American cause; the

Onondaga even brought corn and supplies to General Washington's starving soldiers at Valley Forge. Yet the stupidity of the Continental Army generals, such as Major General Nathanael Greene (1742–1786), in attacking all Haudenosaunee homelands, instead of just those that sided with the British, turned other "friendly tribes" against the Americans. Given that the average life expectancy in post-revolution America (1880) was only in the upper thirties, it stands to reason that a great many people in 1788 had experienced the threat of Indian hostilities their entire lives ("Life Expectancy Graphs" n.d.). These experiences shaped the views toward Indians reflected in the U.S. Constitution and in eighteenth- and nineteenth-century governmental policies.

Article I, Section 8, of the U.S. Constitution gives Congress the authority "to regulate Commerce with foreign Nations, and among the several States, and with Indian Tribes." From this derives the authority to make treaties with the Indian nations within U.S. borders. It does *not* implicitly recognize that Indian nations have the first title to the land, as does the Canadian Constitution, nor as required by signing the terms of the 1783 Treaty of Paris. Instead it left open the issue to negotiators to apply the principle on a tribe-by-tribe basis until *Johnson v. M'Intosh* in 1823. Unfortunately for the Indian nations, U.S. negotiators followed the lead of French and British negotiators before them by playing one tribe off another, using food and threat of military force and withholding small pox vaccinations from tribes that did not bow to U.S. terms (Deloria and Wilkins 1999; Josephy 1991).

In 1824, Congress created the Bureau of Indian Affairs (BIA) and delegated it the powers and responsibilities of negotiating treaties, executing treaty conditions, and managing all Indian welfare matters. Initially, the BIA was placed under the control of the War Department, but eventually it was transferred to the Federal Department of the Interior where it remains today. The BIA today holds authority over the management of all Indian lands and resources, referred to as *Indian Country* (U.S. Department of Justice n.d.). This authority includes the management of all Indian reservation lands (on, below, or above), water, and natural resources (e.g., timber, mineral, mining, oil). It also extends to financial investments and investment properties both on and off reservations that the BIA is obligated to manage in the best interest of the respective tribe or individual Indian allottee. The BIA is responsible for the health, well-being, safety, and welfare of all federally recognized Indian people both on and off reservations (U.S. Department of the Interior 2017).

The BIA control and authority over tribal life and reservation business is directly related to the degree of sovereignty that a tribe enjoys and varies from one tribe to another. *Sovereignty* refers to the degree of autonomy or independence in decision making and actions that a tribe exercises in tribal matters, and freedom from federal, state, or local government interference. Bureau of Indian Affairs and state authority over tribal matters varies as a function of the degree of sovereignty a given tribe exercises. In turn, this is a function of the current treaty terms as recognized by the U.S. government. As discussed in other publications (e.g., Archambeault 2014), sovereignty exists along a continuum. The position that a tribe holds along this continuum dictates the degree of independence and autonomy the tribe has.

On one continuum end are Indian nations with complete autonomy over tribal matters. These can issue passports, driver's licenses, and license plates; and some have applied to be recognized as nations by the UN. They have full discretion in the legal use of U.S. government funds, not otherwise in violation of federal law. They have their own criminal justice systems, among other characteristics of an independent nation. Since 9/11, federal intervention is authorized in case of national emergency.

On the opposite end of the sovereignty continuum are "state-only" recognized tribes that have little or no claim to sovereignty. Heading toward the middle are BIA tribes that were created by presidential or congressional actions but not by treaty; these tribes exercise sovereignty like a U.S. corporation or an incorporated city. Next come a majority of treaty-based BIA tribes spanning both sides of the middle. Federally recognized tribes with minimally altered original treaties exercise more discretion than do tribes with altered treaties, such as the Standing Rock Sioux, whose reservation straddles North and South Dakota and whose original treaty was altered by Congress without tribal consent (DeJong 2015).

The U.S. Constitution is silent on protecting Indigenous rights to historic lands or culture (Deloria and Wilkins 1999). Indians were often viewed as obstacles to western expansion that were to be suppressed, moved, or exterminated. During the nineteenth century, Indians were forced onto reservations, rounded up like cattle, or simply executed. From the 1860s until the 1970s, children were taken from parents and placed in boarding schools to destroy Indian cultures and traditions. Prior to the Indian Child Welfare Act (1978), Indian children were adopted out to or placed with white families. The trafficking in black market Indian babies met the same goals. Over the years, reservation schools were enhanced or closed altogether, allowing Indian children to attend public school (Nies 1996).

RISE AND DECLINE OF THE *NATIVE AMERICAN* LABEL IN THE UNITED STATES

For some American Indians of the 1960s and 1970s, the introduction of the Canadian-inspired label *Native American* offered hope for a better future. U.S. Indian reformers, academics, and politicians seized on the term *Native American* as denoting more respect for Indigenous peoples than the "colonial" word *Indian*. However, in doing so they ignored the sullied meaning of the term *Native American* in U.S. history.

Throughout the 1800s, local and national political groups of U.S.-born white Anglo-Saxon Protestants (WASPs), predominantly male, called themselves "right-born native Americans." The label distinguished them from the hordes of immigrants pouring into America from Europe and other parts of the world. Targets of ethnic and religious condemnation were Irish, Italian, and Polish Catholics; Jews; Mormons; eastern Europeans; and others who did not fit the WASP image. By the mid-1800s "native Americans" formed a national party called the "Know Nothings" and ran on political platforms aimed at halting non-WASP immigration and keeping the "lesser races" (African, Mexican, Indian, and other people of color) in their place while keeping Catholics and Jews from "polluting" the nation. The reference to the "Native Americans" still appears in some white racist literature and propaganda today (see Bennett 1988).

THE 1960S–1970S VIEW OF AMERICAN INDIAN HISTORY: BLEAK AND DISMAL

The nineteenth- and early twentieth-century abuses and neglect of American Indians by the U.S. government and BIA is legendary, well documented, and disgraceful (Josephy1991; Nies 1996). This list is exhaustive and too long to identify in this chapter but, briefly, includes forced removal from homelands; confinement on reservations; starvation and extermination policies; abuse, corruption, and theft by government agents; using BIA authority to steal land from tribes and individuals; use of unannounced enrollment deadlines for registration on rolls and blood quantum policies to cull the numbers of entitled Indigenous people from government rolls; and the intentional denial of vaccines and inoculations and later involuntary sterilization of Indian women as means of population reduction. American Indians were considered "children, wards of the government," having no rights or protections except those the benevolent governing authority deemed necessary to maintain order (Deloria and Lytle 1983; Deloria and Wilkins 1999). There were no redress-of-grievance mechanisms, except within the same system responsible for the control of the "Indian problem."

Indians were not citizens until 1924, although some achieved citizenship after American Indian soldiers distinguished themselves in WWI. Not all states recognized Indians as state citizens until the 1950s. Traditional healing ways and dances were forbidden on reservations until the 1940s, but some tribal knowledge was saved by tribal secret societies and in some families (Archambeault 2009). Tens of thousands of Indians served in WWII, the Korean War, and the Vietnam War. Many of these veterans took advantage of the GI Bill and obtained professional and graduate degrees that influenced their reform actions in the late twentieth century.

After nearly a century of forced incarceration on Indian reservations in the United States, the U.S. government reversed itself under the Eisenhower administration of the 1950s and initiated a number of termination and relocation laws and policies. The BIA began decertifying reservations, in part because the U.S. treasury was almost bankrupt from WWII and Korean War debt; selling off Indian trust lands was a source of revenue for the U.S. government (Deloria and Lytle 1983; Deloria and Wilkins 1999; Nies 1996).

Termination policy continued through the Kennedy and Johnson administrations and was only officially ended under the Nixon administration. The cumulative effects on American Indian populations were surprising to many. Although a few reservations were terminated, most were not. Efforts to move Indians from reservations to the cities where jobs existed and postwar labor was needed started with a trickle in the

1950s but grew into a torrent by the 1960s and continued even after the official termination policies had ended in the 1970s.

Unlike the "Trail of Tears" of the Cherokee, Choctaw, and Creek and the "Long Walk" of the Navajo, Apache, and other nations of the nineteenth century, implementation of the termination policies were arguably more humane. But like prior historical experiences with the U.S. government, implementation of termination policies was haphazard with little coordination or forethought. Thousands of Indian men, women, and families were given tickets and travel money and were promised support and help settling in the big industrial cities. Those who succeeded in finding jobs brought other family to the city, and the pattern was repeated.

The termination policies had several unintended effects on U.S. Indian populations. They created a "pan-urban" Indian political identity that emerged as people from different tribes came to live, work, and pray with urban neighbors from other tribes. In some major cities, this shared pan-Indian urban identity created better-educated and politically savvy American Indian populations. Some neighborhood relationships morphed into mainstream urban Indian community help programs and activities, like those in Minneapolis, New York, and San Francisco. Some morphed into radical political action groups, such as the American Indian Movement (AIM). Whereas fraternal, legal, and social American Indian urban organizations strove to build social bridges for American Indian participation in the dominant American society, radical action groups also brought attention to American Indian issues. Examples of these radical actions were the 1969 seizure of Alcatraz; the 1971 seizure of the BIA headquarters in Washington, D.C.; and the 1973 occupation of Wounded Knee and shootout with federal agents. To AIM members and to some other Indians, the BIA and U.S. government were viewed as occupying forces on Indian lands.

Indians who moved to the cities continued their ties with their reservations, remained on tribal rolls, and often moved back and forth from the "rez" to the city throughout their lives. Urban Indian activities increased public awareness of Indian reservation needs and generated additional resources for reservations. They also reawakened interest in tribal traditions and healing ways. Ironically, however, the rebirth of medicine leaders equipped with traditional tribal knowledge did not occur primarily on reservations or in schools of the 1970s and 1980s. The rebirth also took place in state and federal prisons, which provided Indian cultural classes taught by tribal elders and the use of ceremonies, including sweat lodges and pipe ceremonies (Archambeault 2003, 2006, 2009).

Many 1960s and 1970s reformers viewed the terms *Indian, Indian nation*, and *Indian reservation* as being symbols of colonial repression and servitude, abuse, and neglect. Reformers endorsed the new label of *Native American*, which became the politically correct term.

1980S–1990S: TWO REFORM THRUSTS EVOLVE

From the 1980s forward, reformers took the *Native American* moniker in two seemingly contradictory and often confusing directions. One major thrust involved efforts to reform federal law and government policy for American Indians. Two U.S. senators, Dan Inouye of Hawaii and Ben Nighthorse Campbell from Colorado, led the charge, and others followed (Stevens and Leecy 2012). Several key pieces of legislation passed, including the Indian Gaming Regulatory Act (1988); the Native American Graves Protection and Repatriation Act, known as NAGPRA (1990); the Native American Language Act (1990); the American Indian Trust Fund Management Act (1994); and the National Museum of the American Indian Act (2004). Some legislation initiatives using the *Native American* label continued well into the twenty-first century, such as the Native American Breast and Cervical Cancer Treatment Act (2001) and the Native American Children's Safety Act (2016). The relative success of politicians in gaining political support by titling legislation *Native American* emboldened other political and legislative bodies to push the political envelope of the term.

The second political thrust had nothing to do with improving the lives of American Indians. Instead, these legislative and policy reform efforts were aimed at two goals. First, broadening the meaning of the legal term *Native American* to include other groups of U.S. Indigenous peoples, such as those from Alaska and the Pacific Islands, Native Hawaiians, American Samoans, and others. Second, equating the term *Native American* with the legal status of American Indian, thereby making all Native Americans entitled to the rights, protections, and governmental financial support that are constitutionally reserved for American Indians. In short, the thrust of these efforts was to usurp the constitutional rights, privileges, and financial support of American Indians.

From the late 1990s forward, opposition groups systematically challenged the idea of conferring the legal status and rights constitutionally reserved for American Indians to the Native American label. Court decisions (e.g., *Rice v. Cayetano* 2000), political lobbying, opposition from some tribes, and administrative policy revision finally achieved legal and political clarification on these issues. Efforts to bypass BIA certification failed. Courts and government policymakers agreed with the opposition groups on these points:

- Article 1, Section 8, of the Constitution has been interpreted as not allowing the U.S. government to negotiate with any Indigenous group that is not a federally recognized Indian nation by the BIA.
- The status of Native American is not recognized by the BIA or the federal government as being a legal status, nor is it equal to the legal status of American Indian.
- The application of the Native American terminology to Pacific Islanders or other non-BIA certified groups does not give any of these groups legal status under the U.S. Constitution and current federal laws.

Eventually, many reformers abandoned the *Native American* label. Instead, starting in 2009, legislation began being introduced that uses terms such as Native Hawaiian (Native Hawaiian Government Reorganization Act 2009), Samoan Native, and Virgin Island Native.

TWENTY-FIRST-CENTURY CONFUSION IN THE USE OF *NATIVE AMERICAN* LABEL

After five decades of use and misuse, the term *Native American* has become confusing. On one side, it no longer has a singular connection to American Indians because of its overuse in a broader Indigenous context. Nevertheless, some federal legislation that applies only to American Indians and Alaska Natives is still being enacted by Congress with *Native American* in it.

Most twenty-first-century U.S. federal legislation and policy carefully avoids the use of *Native American* in substantive law. For example, consider the wording in the 2010 Tribal Law and Order Act. Whenever a legal status is referenced, one of these words or phrases is used: *American Indian and Alaska Native, Indian Country, tribal law and justice,* or *tribal member.* The only time *Native American* is used is in an agency letterhead introducing the legislation. Consider also that in its current public information, the U.S. Department of the Interior, Indian Affairs, uses only the *American Indian and Alaska Native* terminology, not *Native American* (U.S. Department of Interior n.d.). Perhaps if ever enacted, correct terminology will be further clarified by the Tribal Recognition Act of 2017 (HR 3744). Government agencies appear to avoid the *Native American* label wherever possible, reserving its use to politicians and public information.

American Indians and Alaska Natives are the only Indigenous people in the United States qualified to negotiate with the U.S. government based on the U.S. Constitution. To be entitled to this legal federal status, a person must be enrolled in a BIA recognized tribe or Alaskan village with headquarters located in Indian Country and be in good standing with that tribe. The rights, protections, and forms of federal support to which a tribal member or Alaskan Native is entitled vary from tribe to tribe, largely influenced by the conditions of the original treaty (or absence of one) with the U.S. government. Individuals can lose their "good standing" for a variety of reasons, including insufficient blood quantum, behavior that is threatening to the tribe, or punitive actions taken by tribal councils. Tribes and villages can lose their BIA recognition for many reasons, such as insufficient numbers of tribal or village members, lost culture, and failure to comply with BIA regulations, among others. Being an Indigenous person or being labeled *Native American* by a state's legislature does not meet these qualifications.

All American Indians and Alaska Natives are Indigenous people, but not all Indigenous people in the United States are American Indian. The use of the term *Native American* often obscures this reality in scholarly and political discussions, particularly where entitlement matters are at issue. There is a much simpler and more accurate terminology that could be used when discussing U.S.-centered issues, the dichotomous classification of BIA certified Indian or non–BIA certified Indian. Immediately, BIA or federally recognized American Indians and village Natives are identified and government and private information about this segment of the U.S. Indigenous population is easily found. But what about the self-labeled American Indians who are non–BIA certified Indians or communities recognized by individual states as being Native American? Who are these people, why do they claim American Indian status, and how many people are there?

There are little actual data available to comprehensively answer these questions. However, after excluding Indian "wannabees," non-BIA Indians in the United States come from several overlapping groups. The following are five such groups: (1) U.S. community groups who are of Indigenous ancestry but who have no status with the United States. Examples include Cajuns in Louisiana; Mestizos from the Southwest United States; some Mission Indians from California, Texas, Arizona, and New Mexico; and state-recognized Indian communities, cultural organizations, and clubs (see 500 Nations 2017). (2) Those who live on or around Indian reservations or Alaskan villages but are not tribally enrolled. (3) The generational descendants of the thousands of Indian babies and children removed from their tribal homes and reared by whites from the 1860s through 1978 when stopped by the Indian Child Welfare Act. (4) Individuals and families whose oral traditions hold that they are American Indians, but there are no documentation links to any ancestor on one of the major Indian rolls. (5) Special communities, such as the Houma Indians in South Louisiana, that, although historical records and cultural traditions are as strong as any federally recognized tribe, have only state recognition because powerful oil, natural gas, and chemical companies control the swampland that would justifiably constitute their reservation and spend millions of dollars lobbying against Houma recognition.

CONCLUSION

This chapter is organized around answering several related questions. Based on the facts and analysis presented, the conclusions seem clear. The descendants of Indigenous peoples in the United States who are BIA recognized and in good standing with their Indian tribe or Alaska Native village are entitled to the legal rights and protections set in motion by Article I, Section 8, of the U.S. Constitution as *Indian tribes*. Other descendants of Indigenous peoples, whether from the United States or any other country, who are not BIA certified are not entitled to the rights and protections due American Indians and Alaska Natives. This includes American Indigenous people such as Native Hawaiians, Samoans, Puerto Ricans, and others. As noted, other laws may apply to these groups, however.

The courts and federal agencies currently hold that the Canadian-inspired term *Native American* is not equivalent to the term *American Indian*, nor does it entitle its holder to any rights, protections, privileges, or support due to American Indians and Alaska Natives. Neither does the UN or Canadian designation of Indigenous peoples entitle the holder to rights and protections due American Indians and Alaska Natives. Finally, the designation by a state recognizing an Indigenous community as being American Indian or Native American does not entitle the holder to the status and protections of American Indians and Alaska Natives.

So, why do so many scholars, politicians, and social action groups and the popular media use *Native American* so extensively, and *Indigenous peoples* occasionally? Is it to protect Indigenous identity, or is it a case of historically blind political correctness out of touch with reality?

A far more accurate terminology for classifying and understanding issues impacting individual U.S. Indigenous populations is to simply dichotomize them into either being BIA certified or non–BIA certified. Far different sets of laws and political circumstances apply to each. Although there are volumes of information on BIA tribes, there is a dearth of information on non-BIA Indigenous communities and individuals. Maybe future research can address relevant issues more precisely by applying this dichotomous classification.

NOTE

1.   Among Native peoples in the United States, common usage varies among the terms *American Indian*, *Native American*, *Indigenous*, and *Native*, with some people preferring one term over the others. In this chapter, terminology focuses on legal usage and legal implications.

REFERENCES

Archambeault, William G. 2003. "Web of Steel and the Heart of the Eagle: The Contextual Interface of American Corrections and Native Americans." *Prison Journal* 83 (1): 3–25.

———. 2006. Imprisonment and American Indian Medicine Ways: A Comparative Analysis of Conflicting Cultural Beliefs, Values, and Practices. In *Native Americans and the Criminal Justice System*, eds. Jeffrey Ian Ross and Larry Gould, 143–60. Boulder, CO: Paradigm.

———. 2009. Search for the Silver Arrow: Assessing Tribal-Based Healing Traditions and Ceremonies in Indian Country Corrections. In *Criminal Justice in Native America*, ed. Marianne Nielsen and Robert Silverman, 191–206. Tucson: University of Arizona Press.

———. 2014. The Current State of Indian Country Corrections. In *American Indians at Risk*, vol. 1, ed. Jeffery I. Ross, 77–94. Santa Barbara, CA: Greenwood Press.

Bennett, David H. 1988. *The Party of Fear: The American Far Right from Nativism to the Militia Movement*. Chapel Hill: University of North Carolina Press.

Corwin, Edward. 1915. "The French Objective in the American Revolution." *The American Historical Review* 1 (1): 22–61.

DeJong, David H. 2015. *American Indian Treaties: A Guide to Ratified and Unratified Colonial, United States, State, Foreign, and Intertribal Treaties and Agreements, 1607–1911*. Salt Lake City: University of Utah Press.

Deloria, Vine, Jr., and Clifford Lytle. 1983. *American Indians, American Justice*. Austin: University of Texas Press.

Deloria, Vine, Jr., and David Wilkins. 1999. *Tribes, Treaties, and Constitutional Tribulations*. Austin: University of Texas Press.

Elbein, Saul. 2017. "'These Are the Defiant 'Water Protectors' of Standing Rock.'" *NG Dispatches*, January 26. http://news.nationalgeographic.com/2017/01/tribes-standing-rock-dakota-access-pipeline-advancement/.

500 Nations. 2017. "State Tribes." http://500nations.com/tribes/Tribes_State-by-State.asp.

Josephy, Alvin M., Jr. 1991. *The Indian Heritage of America*. Boston: Houghton Mifflin.

"Life Expectancy Graphs." n.d. http://mappinghistory.uroregon.edu/english/US/US39-01.html.

National History Day, National Archives and Records Administration and USA Freedom Corps. n.d. "Treaty of Paris (1783)." https://www.ourdocuments.gov/doc.php?flash=true&doc=6.

Nies, Judith. 1996. *Native American History: A Chronology of a Culture's Vast Achievements and Their Links to World Events*. New York: Ballantine Books.

Norton, Rictor. n.d. "Cherokee Delegations to England, 18th Century." Geni. https://www.geni.com/projects/Cherokee-Delegations-to-England-18th-Century/14699.

Online Etymology Dictionary. n.d. http://www.etymonline.com/index.php?term =Indian.

Smith, Caitlin C. M. 2012. "The Jay Treaty Free Passage Right in Theory and Practice." *American Indian Law Journal* 1 (1): 161–80.

Stevens, Ernest L., Jr., and Kevin Leecy. 2012. "Senator Daniel K. Inouye Was One of the Giants of Our Time." Indian Country Today Media Network. http:// indiancountrytodaymedianetwork.com/news/politics/niga-senator-daniel-k -inouye-was-one-of-the-giants-of-our-time-146451.

The Straight Dope. 2001. "Does 'Indian' Derive from Columbus's Description of Native Americans as 'una Gente in Dios'?" http://www.straightdope.com /columns/read/1966/does-indian-derive-from-columbuss-description-of -native-americans-as-una-gente-in-dios.

United Nations Division for Social Policy and Development Indigenous Peoples. n.d. "Indigenous Peoples at the UN." https://www.un.org/development/desa /indigenouspeoples/about-us.html.

U.S. Department of the Interior, Bureau of Indian Affairs. 2017. "Frequently Asked Questions." http://www.bia.gov/FAQs/.

U.S. Department of the Interior, Bureau of Indian Affairs. n.d. *BIA Manual: Indian Affairs*, part 28, chap. 451: 1–6. https://www.bia.gov/cs/groups/xraca /documents/text/idc010213.pdf.

U.S. Department of Justice, Offices of the U.S. Attorneys. n.d. "Indian Country Defined." https://www.justice.gov/usam/criminal-resource-manual-677 -indian-country-defined.

U.S. Department of State, Office of the Historian. n.d. "Treaty of Paris, 1783." https://history.state.gov/milestones/1776-1783/treaty.

Women's Earth and Climate Network. 2016. "15 Indigenous Women on the Front-lines of the Dakota Access Pipeline Resistance." http://www.ecowatch.com /indigenous-women-dakota-access-pipeline-2069613663.html.

Zambelich, Ariel, and Casi Alexandra. 2016. "In Their Own Words: The 'Water Protectors' of Standing Rock." NPR. http://www.npr.org/2016/12/11/505147166 /in-their-own-words-the-water-protectors-of-standing-rock.

LEGAL RESOURCES

American Indian Trust Fund Management Act PL-103-412 (1994).

Daniels v. Canada Indian Affairs and Northern Development, SCC 12 (2016).

Indian Child Welfare Act 25 U.S.C. 1901–63 (1978).

Indian Gaming Regulatory Act PL100-497 (1988).

Johnson v. M'Intosh 21 U.S. 543, 5 L. Ed. 681 (1823).

National Museum of the American Indian Act PL 105-185 (2004).

Native American Breast and Cervical Cancer Treatment Act PL 107-121 (2001).

Native American Children's Safety Act PL 114-165 (2016).

Native American Graves Protection and Repatriation Act PL 101-601 25 USD 3001-3013 (1990).

Native American Language Act PL 101-477 (1990).

Native Hawaiian Government Reorganization Act H.R. 2314, 111th Congress (2009).

Rice v. Cayetano 528 U.S. 495 (2000).

(British) Royal Proclamation (1763).

Treaty of Paris (1763).

Treaty of Paris (1783).

Tribal Law and Order Act 25 U.S.C. 2801 (2010).

Tribal Recognition Act (2017) H.R. 3744.

U.S. Bill of Rights (1791).

U.S. Constitution (1789).

5

"EXERCISING" SOVEREIGNTY

American Indian Collegiate Athletes

ALISSE ALI-JOSEPH

O N APRIL 7, 2013, the Louisville women's basketball team clinched their spot in the NCAA Division I championship game by creating the biggest upset in women's college basketball history.[1] Avid basketball fans were not the only ones glued to ESPN, as American Indians across the nation were cheering on the Schimmel sisters of Louisville. Shoni and Jude Schimmel grew up on the Confederated Tribes of the Umatilla Reservation in eastern Oregon and have become two of the most well-known and talked-about American Indian athletes this decade (Confederated Tribes of Umatilla Indian Reservation/Facebook 2013). Their talent on the court and continuous reference to their Native identity has caught the attention of American Indian people around the country. Although basketball has long been the most popular sport on reservations, and talented American Indian athletes populate reservation and urban communities, seldom does that esteem translate into great performances at the highest college ranks.

In the 2011–2012 academic year, only twenty-one women and four men identified as American Indian/Alaska Native among the 10,151 basketball players at the Division I level (Irick 2011). As Shoni, the star of the team, and Jude, the talented passer and playmaker, took the court in New Orleans, American Indians from around the nation attended in support, holding up signs that read "Rez Girls Rock," "Native Pride," and "Never Give Up." Social media sites[2] filtered hundreds of pictures of the sisters with quotes associating basketball with Native pride: "Shoni and Jude have Louisville playing 'Rez ball,' a ferocious, attacking style of basketball, fueled by passion, creativity, and relentless aggressiveness." The "Schimmel Showdown" craze exemplifies that basketball serves a passionate communal purpose and provides an objective measure of success for players and fans alike. The following statement was circulated around Facebook just minutes before the Schimmel sisters took the court:

> The time has come. The Schimmel Show takes the court in a final four game that pits Louisville against California and the whole nation is watching. Let's all unite, every Indian in the country, everyone, everywhere, let us watch, update and tweet like frenzied warriors. This is history in the making. Get ready to smudge your TVs. Shoni! Jude! Umatilla Thrilla! (ndnsports.com/Facebook 2013)

Although sports may be understood by everyone in the world, it is interpreted very differently, given place and context. This chapter explores the injustices forced upon American Indian youth through educational policies and, more importantly, examines how sport and athletics aid in the agency of American Indian people within both secondary and postsecondary education to "exercise" sovereignty.

"Sport contributes to development" is a popular saying and belief in America today. The pervasiveness of sports in our lives inspires us to "Be Like Mike" and to "Just Do It." Sport icons infuse our televisions and wardrobes and motivate us to both root for our team and play like our heroes. A comprehensive survey by American Sports Data (2000) found that 26.2 million young people aged six to seventeen played on at least one organized sports team. That figure represents 54 percent of the 48.5 million children within that age range in the United States. Another 10 million play team sports, but only in casual pickup situations, not as part of an organized team. Boys' participation totaled 14.7 million and girls' 11.3 million. A similar study conducted five years later showed that among a slightly older age group of ten- to seventeen-year-olds, sports participation had jumped to 59 percent (American Sports Data 2005). Youth sports programs have become infused through small rural towns to big cities not only for the act of "playing" a sport but also to aid in the positive physical and psychological developmental processes of youth.

For American Indian people, sport and physical activity are inherently tied to community. Most American Indian societies have historically placed a high value on physical abilities and competition as means to earn status; honor their families, communities, and deities; and instill discipline and other core values like resilience, hard work, and concentration. Prior to contact with Europeans (precontact) tribes held suites of tribal or intertribal sporting events and contests, which were many times acknowledged as ceremonial. Creation stories, oral histories, and observational reports from travelers and explorers documented extensive and diverse sport activity among many tribes; for example, *ishtaboli* (stickball) within the Choctaw community and lacrosse among the Haudenosaunee communities.

In traditional American Indian societies, running had a prominent role in daily life, often integrating religious, societal, and cultural ideals. Footraces have been the most universal and popular of all Indian sports and games; traditional running activities ranged from informal play among youth to highly organized and ceremonial races of adults, which often involved whole communities. Tribal communities placed great importance on running for reasons unrelated to sports and games; it was recognized that people could be heavily dependent on rapid flight for survival. In addition, a multitude of social concerns and daily demands required Indians to travel great distances under time limitations by foot, the only means of travel available in the years prior to horses and automobiles. Warfare, trade, message delivery, and pursuit of animals for food and resources were only conducted and achieved on foot. Therefore, running, often in the form of running societies, was fundamental to the survival and functionality of a community. Oral tradition and written accounts from the eighteenth and nineteenth centuries provide evidence that there have long been extraordinary running performances of historical importance among American Indians (Oxendine 1988).

Sport is tied to American Indian traditional culture and identity, and the manifestation of American Indian athleticism has become inherent in exercising sovereignty and identity while improving American Indian agency and status within an Americanized system of sports. Traditional sports such as stickball and lacrosse are still practiced today as recognition of cultural identity and sovereignty. However, American Indian people continue to use their inherent connection to sport to translate both skill and the assertion of identity to contemporary American sports. The sports discussed within this chapter have become part of American Indian contemporary culture and sports that American Indians have excelled in and for which they are well known.

It was not until the nineteenth century that American Indian athletes began to emerge at the national level, first through Euro-American accounts of Indigenous cultures, then, and more importantly, in association with the rise of sports in American academic institutions (Bloom 2000). The concept of community involvement and teamwork in games and sports was developed and perfected prior to European contact, yet sports were pivotal in both the assimilation of and resistance by American Indian students in the boarding school era. Sports facilitated opportunities and cultural exchange for American Indian students during a time that aimed to instill Western education to accelerate American Indian cultural extinction (Adams 1995).

A quarter of a century ago, Churchill, Hill, and Barlow observed, "Although it is attempted often enough, it is impossible to consider athletics in North America without addressing the impact of Native American athletes" (King 2005, 132). Athletic prowess became a source of strength and identity for American Indians during their boarding school experience and was quickly transferred to the professional sports world in America. Jim Thorpe, Louis Leroy, Albert Exendine, "Chief" Bender, William "Lone Star" Dietz, and Louis Tewanima, all products of early twentieth-century boarding school athleticism, became popular names across American sports arenas. Moreover, athletics have been central to the historical influence of American Indian education, to interpretations of race and race relations, and the formulations of identity.

Since the emergence of sports as a distinct social domain in North America in the nineteenth century, American Indians have excelled in a multitude of sports including football, baseball, basketball, running, and the Indigenous sport of lacrosse (King 2005, xv), yet they were and continue to be underrepresented in mainstream higher education institutions. The information provided here documents the changing dynamics of American Indian athletes over time.

In 1915, Charles Eastman, a physician and author, surveyed the condition of American Indians in *The Indian To-day* and highlighted the contributions of Indigenous people to the general society:

In the athletic world this little race has no peer, as is sufficiently proven by their remarkable record in football, baseball, and track athletics. From the fleet Deerfoot to this day we boast the noted names of Longboat, Sockalexis, Mebus, Pierce, Frank Hudson, Tewanima, Metoxen, Meyers, Bender, and Jim Thorpe. (King 2005, xi)

Eastman himself exemplifies American Indians emerging into mainstream society, viewing sports as a pathway toward education, assimilation, and equality. The importance of implementing sports in educational institutions had not always been emphasized, however.

The boarding school experiment began in the late nineteenth century as the migration of Europeans and Euro-Americans swept across North America, claiming American Indian lands and leading to the removal of tribes to isolated reservations. One of the primary goals of the federal government was to assimilate American Indians into mainstream society. Carlisle Indian School founder General Richard Henry Pratt's expression "kill the Indian and save the man" became a policy in the late nineteenth and early twentieth centuries. Boarding schools isolated youth from their families and communities. Teachers indoctrinated students with American ideals of individualism, democracy, cooperation, time management, and Christianity. These principles were communicated through the English language and implemented in a militaristic style of physical training (Bloom 2000, xiii, xxi).

It was in this kind of environment that Eastman asked General Pratt why he had not introduced football in his school. Pratt responded, "Why if I did that, half the press of the country would attack me for developing the original war instincts and savagery of the Indian! The public would be afraid to come to our games." Eastman replied, "Major, that is exactly why I want you to do it. We will prove that the Indian is a gentleman and a sportsman" (as quoted in King 2005, xi). During this time, American Indian people had little control over their own lives and were guided by the Western notions of the "savage." American Indian culture both frightened Euro-Americans and limited westward expansion. Therefore, this conversation exemplifies the immense responsibility of the American Indian athlete in the mainstream spotlight; through both his actions and achievements, he could improve the image and perception of all American Indian people, both on and off the athletic playing field.

In *To Show What an Indian Can Do,* Bloom (2000) explores the relationship between sports as a form of popular culture and the politics
of assimilation that characterized boarding school life between 1879
and 1960 in a historical overview. Although reluctant at first, Pratt soon
embraced the promise of sport at Carlisle. In 1897—after he had listened
to Eastman—he stated, "If it was in my power to bring every Indian
into the game of football, to contend as my boys have contended with
the different young men of the colleges, I would do it, and feel that I was
doing them an act of the greatest Christian kindness, and elevating them
from the hell of their home life and reservation degradation into paradise"
(King 2005, xi).

Athletics were then embraced by boarding schools to not only facilitate
assimilation but also to teach young men and women how to respectfully
compete with others. These sports essentially duplicated programs at non-
Indian schools. American Indian students who participated in sports generally excelled athletically, particularly at the Carlisle and Haskell schools
(Bloom 2000). Sports uniquely constituted the cultural politics involved
in federal efforts to educate American Indians and acted as a dynamic
cultural form. This proved to be successful on several levels according to
Bloom (2000, 21):

> Now this Hopi man spoke at a meeting, he spoke about the reservation.
> When he was ten years old, he could run in an open range for miles and
> miles, then later on, they sent him to school and it seems like he was just
> in a closed-in fence or house and a person right there says, "Stand up, sit
> down, go that way, go this way, go to bed, get up." It's like that. And it
> ruined his thinking. He doesn't think any more like an Indian. And he gave
> up and he thought, *well, if I can't have what I had before, I might as well not
> think.* Because thinking as a white person gets mixed up with an Indian.

Although students experienced heartache while away from home,
the athletic assimilation efforts proved not to be successful assimilative
or acculturative strategies on many levels, since most of the basic plays
used today in professional and collegiate football, like the long pass, were
developed by American Indian students and their Native and non-Native
coaches, and were often based on ancestral warfare techniques such as
counting coup (Jenkins 2007). Native students knew this and took pride

in essentially indigenizing American sports and making them their own. They employed creative strategies, and what developed were pan-Indian interactions and economic opportunities for American Indian men, such as Jim Thorpe, Jon Levi, and Charles "Chief" Bender, to play on professional football and baseball teams. Thus, American Indian peoples have played a fundamental role in American athletics, much of it while they were enrolled in schools (Bloom 2000).

Boarding school sports not only helped to promote the educational missions of these institutions by displaying American Indians behaving and competing in a way that was considered civilized and contained, but they also clearly showed how students had the capacity to take advantage of contact spaces, whenever they could find them, and use these zones to their own advantage and as places of resistance. Here they experienced pride, pleasure, and the creative formation of identity as "winners" rather than humanity's predestined "losers." The Carlisle football team used trickery and humor both on and off the field; for example, the theft of tribal lands was a standing source of jokes and humor, one of the few ways in which Natives had to come to grips with what had happened to their peoples. After a bad call from a referee or a racist remark from the opposing team, they would use irony and say, "What's the use of crying about a few inches when the white man has taken the whole country?" (as quoted in Jenkins 2010).

Perhaps no other game embodied the importance sports symbolized to American Indians in the boarding school era more than the 1912 match where the Carlisle Indians faced West Point. On November 9, 1912, the West Point locker room contained nine future generals, including four future World War II generals, as well as future United States president Dwight David Eisenhower, who was known for punishing football opponents. A win would end all argument and establish Carlisle as the best team in the country, as well as symbolize not only American Indian physical prowess but also intelligence in strategic football, thereby beating the white man at his own game. The last death of the Plains' Indians Wars occurred when Plenty Horses, a former student at Carlisle, had gunned down Edward Casey, a former West Point cadet, in January 1891. Just twenty-one years later, American Indians and soldiers were set to square off again, this time "peacefully" on the football field at West Point. In a game that would later be recognized as "The Real War of the West," Jim

Thorpe, in his greatest performance as a college player, led Carlisle to a 22–6 victory (Jenkins 2010).

Football at Carlisle reached a level of success and visibility that had never before, nor since, been attained by an Indian school. The extraordinary achievements of the team from such a small training school against major universities not only were astonishing from a sports standpoint but also captured the imagination of a large segment of the American public (Jenkins 2010, 161–82). The *New York Times* called the Carlisle Indians "one of the most spectacular aggregations of football players, especially in the backfield, ever assembled. The most perfected brand of football ever seen in America" (Rubinfeld 2006, 168).

American Indian females had a somewhat different experience in sports, however, due to the enculturation needs for their expected societal roles and government policies of proper education. Lomawaima (1993, 228) claims that "in order to mold young people's minds, 19th Century educators bent first to mold their bodies according to gender- and race-specific notions of capacities and inclinations." Boys were provided greater opportunity to participate in sports (athletic contests); the orientation of their physical education was also deeply seated in the gender ideologies of boarding schools (masculinity, competitiveness, male solidarity, and physical prowess). The focus on one gender's boarding school experience is motivated by the strict sex segregation enforced in the schools that generated different personal lives for boys and girls. The Victorian "cult of domesticity training for girls was a clear surface manifestation of the gender and race-defined fault lines segmenting American society" (Lomawaima 1993, 227). Female physical fitness heavily emphasized and oriented toward an education in a new identity. For girls, physical education through exercise was displayed through passivity, sexual restraint, domestic femininity, indoor activity, and light exercise (Bloom 2000; Lomawaima 1993). Natural athletic ability and behavior were monitored, reshaped, and even eliminated in order to realign feminine behavior with mainstream, non-Native values.

Girls were limited to dance, gymnastics, and calisthenics because these embodied passivity and sexual restraint (Bloom 2000). Prevailing attitudes regarding women's frailty, inferiority, and the control of female sexuality were translated into the girls' physical education curriculum. This racialized gender hierarchy directly affected not only American Indian females' opportunities to participate in sports during the boarding school era but also the notoriety of American Indian female athletes for the general society. As Jennifer Hargreaves (2000, 1) writes, "A culture is remembered for its heroes and heroines, and sport constructs them and influences our perceptions of them continuously. But heroes are more easily defined than heroines and there is greater social importance attributed to the production and celebration of male heroism." One example is the 1904 girls' basketball team from the Fort Shaw Indian Boarding School in Montana. Basketball became instantly popular with girls and women since it was one of the few active sports deemed acceptable for the "fairer sex" at a time when "strenuous activity" was seen as harmful to female health (Peavy and Smith 2005). The girls' success on the court, however, soon overshadowed this controversy. Since its organization in 1902, the team elicited great school and community pride as they beat most of the state's college and high school teams, and a few boys' teams as well. Their success became so well known that they were invited to the 1904 Louisiana Purchase Exposition in St. Louis as students of the "Model Indian School." The young women from Fort Shaw proved to be worthy ambassadors of their school, their state, and tribes, defeating every team they played and returning home from St. Louis as world champions (Parezo and Fowler 2007; Peavy and Smith 2005). Although women's basketball would not gain notoriety until decades later, the ladies from Fort Shaw overcame barriers of gender, race, and class, while both directly and indirectly disproving stereotypes concerning the athletic, academic, and physical prowess of American Indian females.

Retrospectively, boarding school sports not only helped to promote the educational mission of government institutions by displaying American Indians behaving and competing in a way that was "civilized," but they also clearly showed how students had the capacity to take advantage of spaces whenever they could find them. Unfortunately, while they experienced pride, pleasure, and the creative formation of identity, they also met racism (Bloom 2000). Beyond the schools' policy and practice devoted to domestic education and to the total control of American Indian people, the acute, penetrating focus on girls' attire, conduct, posture, and hairstyles portrayed a racially defined perception of American Indian people's physical bodies as "uncivilized" (Lomawaima 1993, 229).

The introduction of sports as a positive means to education and of the sports arena as a new, more civilized frontier marked a new phase in American Indian education, as well as Indian-white relations; furthermore, they facilitated the integration of American Indian youth from different tribes at the federal boarding schools. Over the course of the twentieth century, sports fostered ethnic identity and pride among American Indian student athletes. Bloom (2000, 37) concludes that boarding school athletic programs "created a context for the celebration of intertribal cooperation and identity, sometimes on a scale rarely ever seen before."

The educational shifts regarding American Indian people reflect federal government policies over time. With the rise of Indian activism in the 1960s and 1970s and an increasing demand for American Indian educational reforms, the 1960s were a particular time of change in Indian education history. The passage of the 1972 Indian Education Act and the 1975 Indian Self-Determination and Education Assistance Act called for American Indian people to take control of their own lives and destiny. Tribal people desired self-determination because the BIA had controlled the direction of formalized schooling for American Indian children for more than a century. Under self-determination, tribes began to take control of the education of their children.

Despite whether physical education is prominent within school settings, interscholastic sports are popular within American Indian communities. In some rural communities, like the Hopi in northeastern Arizona, their running tradition is strong within their school system and supported across their reservation in all communities. The boys' cross-country team at Hopi High School, located in Keams Canyon, has won twenty-six consecutive state championships. In 1990, just three years after the team was created, it won its first state meet, and in 2006, it broke the national record for most consecutive state championships won by a boys' cross-country team. Not only have the young men been successful, the Hopi High School girls' cross-country team too won its sixth straight state championship in 2012, with twenty overall. The secret to the Hopis' success lies in their cultural values and traditions. In a recent ESPN (2016) story "Run Hopi," a member of the boys' team proclaimed, "We do it for our people, our tradition, our culture." Running has its roots in the creation of the universe. Elders tell young people to run early in the morning.

The benefits of running include not only physical health but also spiritual and mental well-being, thus helping individuals and the society to endure (ESPN 2016). The running success at Hopi High School is not a lone occurrence. American Indian running programs are common in high schools, particularly in the Southwest, where running is tied to showing respect for one's culture. Tuba City High School's (located on the Navajo reservation and bordering the Hopi reservation in northeastern Arizona) boys' and girls' cross-country teams have won a combined thirty team and fourteen individual state titles in the past forty years.

Running is not the only sport that highlights the talent of American Indian athletes. Basketball, as mentioned previously, is popular in both rural and urban American Indian communities. Communities are recognizing the importance of promoting and encouraging American Indian youth to become physically active as a way to overcome obesity, diabetes, and chronic diseases triggered by inactivity. A recent story in *Indian Country Today* recognizes that "basketball has become a necessary and relevant piece of Native culture. Granted, it's a *new* piece of our culture, but it is there—like most pieces of our culture—[it] is dedicated to our children's survival. Until we find out *what* those needs are to reinvigorate Indian children's sense of purpose, basketball will have to do" (Ross 2012, n.p.).

Sport is not just a pastime on reservations; it has become a means to promote culture, maintain health, and access education. It has the potential "to raise a generation of leaders by creating the spark that ignites Native American youth to set their sights higher, make the most of their potential and reach their dreams" (NABI 2010, n.p.). The dream of many Native high school athletes is to leave the reservation and succeed in collegiate athletics. Despite the popularity and talent across reservations and cities, there are dishearteningly low numbers of American Indian collegiate athletes.

Barriers to a college education for American Indians have been due to unequal opportunities and discriminatory education practices and policies. Acosta (1980, 52) states that American Indians were the most educationally disadvantaged of all ethnic groups in the nation in the 1970s. Moreover, extensive data reveal that American Indians still represent the lowest percentage of any ethnic group in the United States' higher education system (National Center for Education Statistics 2016). Although progress has been significant, there are numerous barriers American Indians and tribal communities must confront in locating appropriate colleges, gaining admission, matriculating, and then persisting until graduation, and as such, there needs to be further research on how to improve both higher education attendance and graduation rates for American Indian students. This may indicate that community (school, family) involvement in a child's preparation for and retention in college is needed.

Athletics can serve as a pathway toward accessing higher education for American Indians and a means to increase higher education enrollment and graduation rates, while lowering dropout rates. This, in turn, presents the opportunity for a higher income and greater economic opportunities. Although sport is a vehicle by which many promising individuals often seek educational or other opportunities, American Indian students are less likely than any other ethnic group in the United States to play a collegiate sport (National Collegiate Athletic Association 2015). In the 1970s, specific data concerning contemporary American Indian collegiate athletes were almost nonexistent. Today, the figures are unfortunately not much different. For example, in *The 2010 Racial and Gender Report Card: College Sport* compiled by the Institute for Diversity and Ethics in Sport (Lapchick 2010), American Indians were not mentioned once in the sixty-seven-page document. Although it suggests that college sports substantially improved racial hiring practices, as well as made progress in gender hiring practices, American Indians were once again left out of the equation.

In 1990, the NCAA began collecting annual ethnic and gender demographic data on each member institution through the NCAA Certification of Compliance form. For the past seventeen years, American Indian and Alaska Native collegiate athletes continue to be underrepresented and reflect disproportionately low numbers for their percentage of the general population and for students attending college. In 2014–2015, American Indians accounted for the lowest percentage of student athletes, with only four-tenths of a percent in all three of the NCAA divisions (0.2 percent for American Indian men and 0.2 percent for American Indian women). Although one would expect low numbers given the American Indian population size in the United States, American Indian collegiate athletes are below parity (0.4 percent participation versus 2.1 percent population) (National Collegiate Athletic Association 2016). Moreover, given the talent of American Indian athletes and popularity of sports within Native communities, these low numbers are even more unfortunate.

From 1999 to 2015, both American Indian men and women represented the lowest percentage of student athletes in NCAA Divisions I, II, and III. In 2015, American Indian men and women represented the lowest numbers (1,901 out of 489,698) of student athletes across all three divisions; black men and women were the second highest represented (68,256), behind only white women and men (319,517) (National Collegiate Athletic Association 2015). In the 2014–2015 breakdown by gender, there were only 1,031 NCAA American Indian/Alaska Native male athletes, compared to 46,701 black male athletes and 175,496 white male athletes. That same year there were 870 American Indian/Alaska Native female athletes, 21,555 black female athletes, and 144,021 white female athletes (National Collegiate Athletic Association 2015).

American Indian/Alaska Native administrators and coaches are also underrepresented within the NCAA. In 2014–2015 there were only two directors of athletics, forty head coaches (thirty-three men and seven women), and 104 staff personnel (fifty-eight men and forty-six women). Only 0.7 percent of all head coaching positions for men's teams were filled by people of color, excluding African Americans (.07 percent American Indian/Alaska Native, 0.8 percent Asian, 1.3 percent Hispanic/Latino, and 0.8 percent Native Hawaiian). For women's teams, American Indian/Alaska Natives held 0.1 percent of head coaching positions. The assistant coach and administrative demographics in all three divisions similarly express the dominant numbers of whites and African Americans. American Indian/Alaska Natives only make up 0.1 percent of assistant coaches for men's teams and 0.1 percent for women's teams in all three divisions. For all administrative positions, American Indian/Alaska Natives only held 0.2 percent of Division I, II, and III positions (National Collegiate Athletic Association 2015).

Although racial and ethnic minorities in administrative and coaching positions have increased over the past seven years, there is a relatively low percentage of American Indian administrative staff and head and assistant coaches compared to other minorities. This affects the access gap American Indians face within every athletic facet of higher educational institutions. With the low percentages of American Indian athletes, in combination with the lack of literature and scholarship representing the

American Indian collegiate athlete experience, American Indian athletes seem somewhat invisible within the sports world. Although the current statistics in collegiate sport continue to make the American Indian collegiate athlete insignificant, American Indian athletes are pursuing sport in college and are motivated by sports to earn degrees.

Participation in sports provides opportunities for athletes not available to other college students. Sport is a vehicle for college admittance, whether athletes desire to obtain just a general education, specialize in a field of study, or attend college solely to play the sport in which they excelled in high school. Sweeney Windchief (Fort Peck Assiniboine), a former collegiate wrestler, believes that sport constitutes "a pretty special place because sometimes it transcends typical race relations than you would normally see. It is a place where you are respectful of each other's differences and are working towards the same thing" (personal communication, October 15, 2012). For Sweeney, sports occupy a special place in his life, as "it really was a unique opportunity for all of us to get to know each other and to set aside some of our stereotypes and our bias." Yet, as sport is celebrated as a path to racial equality and an arena for multicultural understanding in America, racial ideologies continue to shape the ways in which individuals and institutions play, watch, describe, organize, and imagine sports (King 2005, 212). The hardiness of racism has profound implications for the representation of American Indian athletes.

When American Indian athletes become the subject of public discussion they all too often get lost in Euro-American preoccupations and values (King 2005). The 2009 *Denver Post* article "Sporting Dreams Die on the 'Rez'" by Kevin Simpson, like Selena Roberts's 2001 *New York Times* article "Off-Field Hurdles Stymie Indian Athletes," nicely illustrate this pervasive pattern. Both Simpson and Roberts reported on American Indian athletes, focusing primarily on the obstacles that prevent them from excelling in the academic and professional realms: the influence of drugs and alcohol, prejudice and misunderstanding, lack of opportunity, coaches unwilling to recruit athletes from reservations, the isolation of reservation communities, athletes' attachment to family and community, the suppression of individualism, jealousy and conflict within Indigenous communities, and the inability to adjust to white institutions and expectations (King 2005, xxiv). Simpson (2009, 287) reports an example of a coach speaking about one of his American Indian recruits: "'I hate to stereotype,' said Paulsen [coach], 'but is he the typical Indian kid? If Willie [athlete] comes and doesn't make it, nobody will be surprised. My concern is that he'll go home for the weekend and say he'll be back Monday. Which Monday?'" Simpson (2009, 287) goes on to say, "Talented Indians are diverted from their academic and athletic career courses. They are sucked back to subsistence-level life on the reservation by the vacuum created by inadequate education and readily available escapes like drugs and alcohol."

This limiting and frankly biased picture that focuses on difficulties and potential obstacles defines American Indian athletes as "missed opportunities" rather than athletes. Roberts notes that with the exception of Jim Thorpe, Billy Mills, and Notah Begay, "Native American athletes have not made the leap to the highest level of American sport" (as quoted in King 2005, xxiv). Although Simpson and Roberts are right to direct attention to the seeming absence of American Indian athletes on people's top 100 athletes lists, they show a very limited knowledge of the many Indigenous men and women who have participated and excelled in sports at the intercollegiate, professional, and international levels. There have been over two hundred athletes over the last century who competed at the highest levels (King 2005; Oxendine 1988).

NDNsports.com, a website created by two former American Indian college students to promote awareness to the public and Native community online of Native American athletes competing in a wide variety of college and professional sports, currently displays twenty-eight professional American Indian athletes. While searching other websites, I found more than twenty-eight, especially when minor league and amateur teams were included in the criteria.

It is possible to narrow searches too far and basically define Native Americans out of inclusion. To claim that there have only been three successful "big league" athletes not only is misleading, it also suggests that only athletes who become famous or nationally known matter, thus "neglecting in the process the numerous local contexts in which Native Americans play sports and what that participation means to the athletes and their communities" (King 2005, xxv). One of the central tenets of the academic discipline of applied Indigenous studies is that local situations are incredibly important for understanding Native communities and their cultures. It is the communities, not the celebrity's success, that matter; they are the role models for this and the next generation. Sports and activity do matter, but not so much for winning an Olympic gold medal or being considered the best in the world.

As King (2005, 248) concludes, "Too often ignored in sports studies and public culture, Native American athletes deserve, nay demand, attention." When athletes have been featured in the literature, they have normally been presented as passive subjects of a powerful infrastructure. They are portrayed as commodities, alienated and exploited individuals, because they are part of victimized groups. One does not get the story of resilience and endurance because the richness and complexity of these individuals' daily lives are often lost. Scholarship must attend and interrogate identity and culture, exchanges and appropriations, assimilation and resistance, as well as sport as a facet of resilience. In order to fully appreciate the articulations of race, power, and negotiation in sport, American Indians and American Indian identity must be considered; race relations must go beyond the black and white binary. In many ways, sport has been defined as a Euro-American domain, and many scholars are not aware of the rich heritage and lasting contributions of Indigenous peoples and communities, as well as of sport's connection to important issues such as policy, economics, sovereignty, self-determination, and spirituality. More importantly, sport creates opportunities for accomplishment for one's self, family, and community.

Today, a common misconception about American Indian people is that their race, ethnicity, family structure, and economic status are the major factors affecting their success or failure in school and, ultimately, life. This misconception leads educators and others to view Native people as coming from such deficient circumstances that they cannot be expected to thrive. This remains true for the American Indian collegiate athlete. The minimal literature dealing with them aims to victimize and criticize American Indian culture and people as a justification for why there are so few American Indian collegiate athletes. King (2005, xxv) concludes that contemporary literature surrounding Native athletes reiterates the classic lament, "Lo, the poor Indian," as authors confine them (and Indigenous people more generally) within stories of tragedy (missed opportunities, premature deaths, unfulfilled dreams) and descriptions of desolation and disadvantage (the reservation and its social problems). As American Indian athletes maneuver through college, the literature suggests that they do not have any means to assert agency and they simply "return home"

(Simpson 2009). However, Bloom (2000), Gems (2005), and King (2005) conclude that "Native Americans have long used sport as a means to achieve a sense of pride, self-esteem, and respect" (Gems 2005, 1).

During the boarding school era, athletes opened a space in which American Indians could extract symbolic revenge. Bloom (2000, 54) notes that within boarding schools, "to play and beat white teams was even a higher achievement." During this era then, American Indian athletes fostered ethnic identity and pride, served as role models, and evoked great joy and happiness in the midst of grave adversity. American Indian boarding school athletes were resilient, bridging cultures and adapting to or adopting the dominant norms when necessary or beneficial (Gems 2005, 3). Sport served as a meeting place for transformation and persistence; for distinct, even mutually exclusive Indian and white interpretations; and for shared understandings.

Similar to boarding school athletes, contemporary American Indian collegiate athletes express their ability to become stronger through resilient adaptation by learning new skills, developing creative ways of coping, and meeting and overcoming life's challenges. American Indian athletes express agency and resilience through sport by exerting pride in their American Indian identities, forging new relationships and friendships with coaches and teammates, continuing their education after their athletic career concludes, and acting as sources of strength to their own communities and American Indian athletes of all ages. The importance of family, community, and overall Native cultural values and identity are critical elements in their ability to be resilient.

Sports transcend beyond the playing field for American Indian people. As they grow up involved in these activities, athletics becomes an integral aspect of their lives, not separated from their personal development. Sports inspire personal empowerment and the formulation of life skills, which are "those internal personal assets, characteristics and skills such as goal setting, emotional control, self-esteem, and hard work ethic that can be facilitated or developed in sport and are transferred for use in non-sport settings" (Gould and Carson 2008, 60). Because life skills are "taught not caught," the very act of playing sports fosters self-discipline, self-efficacy, teamwork, confidence, work ethic, leadership, and resilience. For American Indian athletes, sport additionally becomes an avenue to connect community with higher education and "exercise" sovereignty.

Although articles have been written about athletes in their tribal communities, these sources often have limited circulation or have tribal-specific distribution. This has allowed the athletes to be known and respected within their communities, but they remain essentially unknown outside of them and continue to lack opportunity to pursue a college education. Even in works specifically dedicated to the American Indian mascot issue and collegiate athletes in general, American Indian collegiate athletes are nearly nonexistent as a topic of discussion. Maybe these voices have been silent because very few have been asked to share their knowledge, perspectives, and experiences. It is time—well past time—to end the silence and positively address this disparity and to collect their stories to give voice to those narratives and then analyze this information to place it within the broader context of the American Indian higher education experience.

NOTES

1.   This chapter is based on original dissertation research from the University of Arizona completed in April 2013. The title of the dissertation is "American Indian Collegiate Athletes: Accessing Education Through Sport."

2.   For American Indian youth, similar to youth across the world today, social media has become a prevalent and popular form of expression. Research and visibility concerning American Indian athletes has unfortunately remained minimal. However, with the use of social media, American Indian people are increasingly able to see, experience, and communicate with and about their sports heroes. American Indian people are able to connect with their role models, express their opinions, and validate the importance of seeing an American Indian person in a positive spotlight through forms of social media such as Facebook.

REFERENCES

Acosta, R. V. 1980. "Minorities in Sports: Educational Opportunities Affect Representation." *Journal of Physical Education, Recreation & Dance* 57 (2): 52–55.

Adams, D. W. 1995. *Education for Extinction: American Indians and the Boarding School Experience, 1875–1928*. Lawrence: University of Kansas Press.

American Sports Data. 2000. *American Team Sports: A Status Report*. Hartsdale, NY: Author.

American Sports Data. 2005. *American Team Sports: A Status Report.* Hartsdale, NY: Author.

Bloom, J. 2000. *To Show What an Indian Can Do: Sports at Native American Boarding Schools.* Minneapolis: University of Minnesota Press.

Confederated Tribes of Umatilla Indian Reservation/Facebook. 2013. https://www .facebook.com/CTUIR.

ESPN. 2016. "Run Hopi." https://www.espnfrontrow.com/2016/07/sundays-sc -featured-tells-story-of-hopi-reservation-cross-country-dynasty/.

Gems, G. R. 2005. Negotiating a Native American Identity Through Sport: Assimilation, Adaptation, and the Role of the Trickster. In *Native Athletes in Sports and Society*, ed. C. R. King, 1–21. Lincoln: University of Nebraska Press.

Gould, D., and S. Carson. 2008. "Life Skills Development Through Sport: Current Status and Future Directions." *International Review of Sport and Exercise Psychology* 1 (1): 58–78.

Hargreaves, J. 2000. *Heroines of Sport: The Politics of Identity.* London: Routledge.

Irick, E. 2011. "NCAA Race and Gender Demographics, 1995–2011." Indianapolis, IN: National Collegiate Athletic Association. http://web1.ncaa.org/rgdSearch /exec/main.

Jenkins, S. 2007. *The Real All Americans: The Team That Changed a Game, a People, a Nation.* New York: Doubleday.

Jenkins, S. 2010. "The Team that Invented Football." Sports Illustrated Vault. http://sportsillustrated.cnn.com/2007/more/04/19/carlisleo423/index.html.

King, C. R. 2005. *Native Athletes in Sport & Society: A Reader.* Lincoln: University of Nebraska Press.

Lapchick, R. 2010. "The 2010 Racial and Gender Report Card: College Sport." The Institute for Diversity and Ethics in Sport. http://web.bus.ucf.edu /documents/sport/2010.pdf.

Lomawaima, K. T. 1993. "Domesticity in the Federal Indian School: The Power of Authority over Mind and Body." *American Ethnologist* 20 (2): 1–14.

NABI Foundation. 2010. http://www.nabifoundation.org/.

National Center for Education Statistics. 2016. "Status and Trends in the Education of American Indians and Alaskan Natives." https://nces.ed.gov/pubs2016 /2016007.pdf.

National Collegiate Athletic Association. 2015. "Sport Sponsorship, Participation and Demographics Search." http://web1.ncaa.org/rgdSearch/exec/main.

National Collegiate Athletic Association. 2016. "Sport Sponsorship, Participation and Demographics Search." http://web1.ncaa.org/rgdSearch/exec/main.

ndnsports.com/Facebook. 2013. https://www.facebook.com/pages/ndnsportscom /195370210570314?fref=ts.

Oxendine, J. B. 1988. *American Indian Sports Heritage*. Champaign, IL: Human Kinetics.

Parezo, N. J., and D. D. Fowler. 2007. *Anthropology Goes to the Fair: The 1904 Louisiana Purchase Exposition*. Lincoln: University of Nebraska Press.

Peavy, L. S., and U. Smith. 2005. World Champions: The 1904 Girls' Basketball Team from Fort Shaw Indian Boarding School. In *Native Athletes in Sports and Society*, ed. C. R. King, 40–79. Lincoln: University of Nebraska Press.

Roberts, S. 2001. "In the Shadows: A Special Report; Off-field Hurdles Stymie Indian Athletes." *New York Times*, June 7. http://www.nytimes.com/2001/06/17/sports/in-the-shadows-a-special-report-off-field-hurdles-stymie-indian-athletes.html.

Ross, G. 2012. "Indians Already Have a Whole Bunch of Sacred Things: We'll Just Call Basketball Really Important." Indian Country Today Media Network. http://indiancountrytodaymedianetwork.com.

Rubinfeld, M. 2006. "The Mythical Jim Thorpe: Re/representing the Twentieth Century American Indian." *International Journal of the History of Sport* 23 (2): 167–89.

Simpson, K. 2009. Sporting Dreams Die on the "Rez." In *Sport in Contemporary Society: An Anthology*, ed. D. S. Eitzen, 285–91. Boulder, CO: Paradigm.

PART III

COMMUNITY RESPONSES

INTRODUCTION BY MARIANNE O. NIELSEN AND KAREN JARRATT-SNIDER

One of the important themes in the chapters in part III is how Indigenous communities use the law and justice system to respond to issues of crime and social justice. There is a great deal of irony in this since, more than any other disadvantaged group in the United States, American Indians have laws that affect only them. This is also the case for Aboriginal peoples in Canada, Indigenous Australians, and Maori in New Zealand/ Aotearoa. The use of law by colonizers is an essential part of the colonialism process. Historically, law legitimized the deprivation of human rights, the theft of land resources, the kidnapping of children into boarding schools, the concentration of American Indian people on resource-poor and much-too-small reservations, and even the killing of Indigenous people and peoples.

Today, the law continues to disadvantage American Indian peoples by limiting their ability to make decisions about their own communities and lives, despite the guarantees of continuing sovereignty made in the original treaties with the American colonial government. Despite centuries of broken treaties by the colonial government, the treaties are still in effect today, as agreements between sovereign nations. Discriminatory federal laws have given control of many aspects of Indigenous lives to the federal government; Public Law 280 states where the federal government has transferred to states criminal and in some cases civil jurisdiction "over some reservations regardless of the Indians' preference" (Getches, Wilkinson, and Williams 1993, 479). The purpose of these laws remains unchanged: theft of resources, assimilation of Indigenous cultures, and social control of people trying to assert their human rights.

Nevertheless, one way to challenge laws is by using laws. In the 1970s, the federal government passed a series of pro-sovereignty laws that restored to some extent American Indian autonomy in many areas, including education and justice. Hiraldo gives an overview of both discriminatory and pro-sovereignty laws as they relate to the welfare of Indian children. She points out that state-recognized tribes do not have the same legal protections as federally recognized tribes. This focus is an important one because of the sixty-six state-recognized tribes in ten states (National Conference of State Legislatures [NCSL] 2016) and the approximately 160 nations that have neither state nor federal recognition (Giese 1997). The state-recognized tribes of North Carolina used the federal Indian Child Welfare Act to negotiate with the state to better protect Native American children from being placed outside the community in foster care because as a state-recognized tribe, their children were not afforded federal protections. Hiraldo describes a process that could serve as a model for unrecognized nations to work with their states to develop legislation to protect not only their children but perhaps their communities and resources.

Luna-Gordinier discusses a different process of using the law to protect American Indian communities and individuals. She describes how American Indian nations have used the Tribal Law and Order Act (2010) and the Violence Against Women Act (2013) to create and enforce culturally appropriate legislation about stalking. First, however, she shows how necessary it is to understand the historical laws and government Indian policy that have limited the power of American Indian nations to protect their female citizens against criminal acts.

As Luna-Firebaugh and Luna-Gordinier illustrate in their chapter on juvenile justice programs in Arizona and Aotearoa/ New Zealand, the assertion of sovereignty does not have to rely on the law; it can also occur at the programmatic level. Community involvement and cultural principles incorporated into effective justice programs, in this case for youth, are a de facto exercise of sovereignty. De facto sovereignty can be limited, however, by restrictive legislation, as has been occurring more frequently in the United States.

REFERENCES

Getches, David H., Charles F. Wilkinson, and Robert A. Williams, Jr. 1993. *Cases and Materials on Federal Indian Law*, 3rd ed. St. Paul, MN: West.

Giese, Paula. 1997. "U.S. Federally Non-Recognized Indian Tribes— Index by State." http://www.kstrom.net/isk/maps/tribesnonrec .html#top.

National Conference of State Legislatures (NCSL). 2016. "Federal and State Recognized Tribes." http://www.ncsl.org/research/state-tribal -institute/list-of-federal-and-state-recognized-tribes.aspx.

6

STALKING IN INDIAN COUNTRY

Enhancing Tribal Sovereignty Through
the Tribal Law and Order Act and the
Violence Against Women Act

ANNE LUNA-GORDINIER

D OMESTIC AND STALKING VIOLENCE are complex problems that
pervade American society. Across all racial groups, violence against
women is primarily domestic: 64 percent of women who reported
being raped, physically assaulted, and/or stalked since age eighteen were
victimized by a current or former husband, cohabiting partner, boyfriend,
or date (Tjaden and Thoennes 2000, iv). American Indian and Alaska
Native women aged eighteen and over are stalked at a rate of 2.2 percent,
the highest of any racial or ethnic group (Catalano 2012). At least 70 percent of the perpetrators of violent crimes against American Indians are
non-Indians (Greenfeld and Smith 1999, vi) American Indian/Alaska
Native women experience violent victimization at a greater rate than any
other racial group (Tjaden and Thoennes 2000, 22). Indigenous Americans are 2.4 times as likely to experience violent crimes and at least twice
as likely to experience rape or sexual assault crimes as compared to all
other races (Greenfeld and Smith 1999, iii). This is particularly troubling
because prior to colonization, domestic violence was uncommon in traditional Native cultures (Murray 1998, 5). Some explanation for this dis-
connection lies in the understanding that the imposition of hierarchical
legal and social structures tied the hands of tribes to do what is right for
their own people.

Federal Indian law and policy has created complicated criminal jurisdictional issues, making it difficult for tribes to maintain law and order
on their lands. In addition, the scant allocation of resources for tribal

criminal justice systems makes law enforcement especially burdensome. Regardless of the causal factors, comprehensive federal legislation to support tribal criminal justice systems is needed. Instrumental in encouraging a more coherent federal response, researchers produced the *Maze of Injustice* report wherein they reframed the problem of sexual violence in Indian Country as an international human rights issue (Amnesty International 2007). The Violence Against Women Act (VAWA) and the Tribal Law and Order Act (TLOA) empower tribes to once again create and enforce culturally appropriate modes of resolution. TLOA acknowledges that tribal justice systems are often the most appropriate institutions for maintaining law and order in Indian Country. Its purpose is to empower tribal governments to effectively provide public safety and reduce the prevalence of violent crime in Indian Country. Once tribes set about creatively using VAWA and TLOA, they may develop a multitude of tactics to not only address domestic violence and stalking on the reservation but also further tribal sovereignty. The methods most likely to be successful are those rooted in tribal values and traditions. Tribes should incorporate these considerations into codes, protocols, training, and prevention programs to ensure that they play an integral part in law enforcement. This will promote law and order on the reservation and help to further tribal sovereignty.

CRIMINAL JUSTICE AND
VIOLENCE AGAINST WOMEN

Stalking and domestic violence present a complex problem for victims and the criminal justice system because the behavior may consist of a series of ongoing noncriminal and criminal acts. In the case of stalking, when these noncriminal acts are taken into account together, they put the victim in a permanent state of physical and mental onslaught (Stevenson 1997, 7). Stalking and domestic violence often further victimize people by restricting their access to usual activities such as maintaining a job or sending their children to school. This cycle of control extends to poor use of law enforcement as well.

According to a National Violence Against Women (NVAW) survey, only 55 percent of women victims reported stalking to the police (Atwell

2002, 83). In addition to the victimization resulting from domestic vio-lence and stalking, victims are further stressed by the rigors of the criminal justice system. Stalking, like "the gendered crimes of rape and domes-tic violence . . . depends on evidence of victim noncompliance with the defendant and evidence that the victim did not precipitate or encourage the defendant's behavior" (Dunn 2002, 3). The actions and character of the victim are often a focus of scrutiny leading to further frustration with law enforcement (Dunn 2002, 2). This creates a barrier to resolution even while the primary victimization continues unabated. Deer (2003/2004) asserts that recognizing and restoring the dignity of victims is the best way to address sexual assault of Indigenous women. There is a dearth of research focusing on stalking, and it has only recently been addressed as a critical social problem (Bachman, Zaykowski, Kallmyer, Poteyeva, and Lanier 2008). Few tribes have the legal codes in place to adequately address stalking and domestic violence. This is perhaps because their cul-tures were forced to change rapidly to accommodate new social ills that had been under control through traditional means.

HISTORY OF FEDERAL INDIAN POLICY

Rather than focusing on reactionary measures to domestic violence, tribal societies were more likely to focus on prevention from the beginning. This was enforced and perpetuated by community and familial accountability. This is not to say that remedies for persistent and irredeemable behav-ior did not exist, however. Varying approaches to domestic regulation reflected the traditions, religious beliefs, and governmental structures of each society (Murray 1998, 8). Regardless of the approach, it is certain that tribal nations and families once successfully regulated issues of violence in their own culturally specific ways. For example, in traditional Southern Cheyenne society, which is usually viewed as patriarchal, marriage was a contract with courtship and gift exchanging. The extended courtship period allowed the girl's older brother, who probably arranged the mar-riage, to make sure he had made a good choice for his sister (Murray 1998). Once married, a woman had a considerably strong position. Wife abuse was grounds for divorce and the woman could either go stay with her family or have a relative declare her divorced and force the husband to leave home. Also lessening the incidence of abuse was matriarchal ownership of property. "If a woman divorced her husband, she had legal claim to the home, its contents, and the children" (Llewellyn and Hoebel 1941, 212–13). The husband also gave up all rights to inheritance from his ex-wife if she died first.

Another example is matrilineal Cherokee society, in which domestic violence was extremely uncommon. Cherokee society emphasized equality, individual freedoms, and personal rights. Unlike almost any other society, the Cherokee had no formal marriage ceremonies, no engagement contracts, and no arranged marriages (Llewellyn and Hoebel 1941). Marriage was not legally binding on husbands or wives; it occurred just by living together, and divorce occurred by moving out. A woman had property rights and she and her clan were responsible for child-rearing. In the case of divorce, the kids stayed with their mother and she sought the aid of brothers for support and protection. "Complementarity of gender roles and statuses among the Cherokee reflect a more open, egalitarian system in which differences in prestige and power reflect individual achievement and age" (Llewellyn and Hoebel 1941, 7). These varying approaches to domestic regulation reflect the traditions, religious beliefs, and governmental structures of diverse societies (Llewellyn and Hoebel 1941, 8). Their social and legal institutions emphasized the prevention of family violence from the beginning.

Unlike the Cherokee, the Cheyenne also devised reactive methods for dealing with abusive husbands. Tribes could benefit from adapting traditional measures to new antiviolence codes to reinforce their cultures and tribal sovereignty.

Integral to addressing the issues around violence against Indian women is an understanding of the complex legal issues surrounding tribal jurisdiction. Tribes once exerted full sovereignty over their land, government, and people; however, their powers have been whittled away over time, which has hampered tribes from exercising control over their reservations in culturally compatible ways.

The current era of American Indian self-determination in federal Indian policy has led to renewed control over reservation resources and governance. However, the U.S. Supreme Court's Indian Country criminal and civil jurisdictional model radically cut back on the rights of tribes to regulate activities by non-Indians on the reservation. Treaties are an uncertain basis for tribal sovereignty in the United States. Most areas of tribal life, including law enforcement, economic development, and governance, are affected by these decisions. For tribes to resolve these problems, they have had to seek new avenues for resolution.

Tribal control over reservation law and order is imperative for tribal sovereignty and is one of the few areas where tribal jurisdiction has been upheld. To succeed, tribes must balance the goals of tribal sovereignty with state and federal needs for accountability in an increasingly hostile legal environment. In many areas tribes have been shackled by federal government bureaucracies. In addition, stalking is particularly trouble-some due to complications arising from jurisdictional conflicts among border towns and reservations. However, new avenues for cooperation have allowed tribes to take control over many of their resources. The Indian Self-Determination and Education Assistance Act of 1975 gave tribes the authority to contract for and receive grants from the direct operation of Department of Interior and Health and Human Services programs serving their tribal members. Under the act, tribal programs are funded by the federal government, but the programs are planned and administered by the tribes themselves. Some tribes have implemented reforms that bypass the Bureau of Indian Affairs (BIA), streamline tribal committees, and increase accountability.

An extremely important aspect of federal Indian law is that although policy has shifted, many of the statutes passed in each previous policy era were never overturned. This often runs to the detriment of tribes, so tribes have sought other avenues to address their concerns.

Congress has regularly responded to issues around criminal jurisdiction in Indian Country by passing piecemeal legislation focused on specific issues. The nature of the law or policy is directed by the political climate at the time. Major laws affecting criminal jurisdiction include the General Crimes Act (1817) that established federal jurisdiction over crimes committed in Indian Country, the Assimilative Crimes Act (1825) that established state laws were applied in Indian Country if no federal laws existed, and the Major Crimes Act (1885) that established federal jurisdiction over serious crimes committed on Indian land. Two subsequent acts that impacted jurisdiction in Indian Country are Public Law 280 (PL 280) (1953) that shifted the responsibility over some Indian tribes to state jurisdictions and the Indian Civil Rights Act (1968) that basically imposed the legally restrictive U.S. Bill of Rights on Indian tribes. Several important legal cases also further restricted Indian criminal jurisdiction, including the infamous *Duro v. Reina* (1990) case that removed tribal jurisdiction over nonmember Indians on the reservation (it was later "fixed" by Congress). Given all the restrictions these laws imposed on Indian jurisdiction, tribes found themselves unable to adequately maintain law and order on their lands. The confusion over who would exercise jurisdiction—the nation, the federal government, or state governments—lack of funding, and remote locations in Indian Country all work to undermine public safety. Particularly affected were American Indian women. For tribes to resolve these problems, they have had to seek new avenues. The Tribal Law and Order Act and the Violence Against Women Act provide some potential opportunities.

TRIBAL LAW AND ORDER ACT

In response to these jurisdictional gaps and the devastating crime rate in Indian Country, Congress passed the Tribal Law and Order Act (TLOA) of 2010. The congressional intent of TLOA is to guarantee tribal criminal justice, expand federal responsibility over Indian Country, improve law enforcement on Indian lands, and enhance tribal sentencing authority. TLOA also established the Indian Law and Order Commission (ILOC) composed of nine volunteer members responsible for conducting a comprehensive study of criminal justice and law enforcement in Indian Country.

COOPERATION AND COORDINATION

Historically, federal prosecutors have regularly declined to prosecute criminal cases in Indian Country. For example, from 2005 to 2009, federal prosecutors declined to prosecute 40 percent of nonviolent cases and 52 percent of violent cases in Indian Country (Government Accounting Office [GAO] 2010, 3). To make matters worse, tribes often do not receive notification of the declinations. This is problematic because while tribes wait to hear back, evidence may be lost or damaged or federal witnesses may become unavailable. Even when a tribal court is able to hear a case, sentencing restrictions limit the penalties for serious crimes. Certainly something needs to be done to promote public safety in Indian Country.

Section 212 of TLOA amends the Indian Civil Rights Act and requires federal actors conducting investigations on tribal land to coordinate with tribal agencies in cases of declinations or nonreferrals of criminal investigations. This coordination also encompasses the use of relevant evidence in tribal court as well as status updates on investigations. In addition, the U.S. Attorney's Office and the FBI are required to report to Congress about declinations of prosecution. The expectation is that the annual reporting requirement will decrease the rate of cases that go unresolved in Indian Country. In addition, the U.S. Bureau of Prisons must now notify tribal law enforcement whenever a prisoner convicted of drug trafficking, a sex offense, or a violent crime is released into Indian Country.

TLOA also requires U.S. Attorney's Offices with jurisdiction in Indian Country to appoint special assistant U.S. attorneys to work as tribal liaisons to promote the prosecution and coordination of cases. TLOA also authorizes the use of tribal prosecutors for this purpose. The goal is for increased coordination of cases and for tribal prosecutors to receive additional support and training. It is anticipated that these special prosecutors will increase the number of federal prosecutions in Indian Country resulting in enhanced public safety.

TRIBAL POLICING, TRAINING, AND CROSS-DEPUTIZATION

The piecemeal history of federal Indian law makes criminal jurisdiction in Indian Country extremely convoluted. Law enforcement officers must unravel these tangled issues while working in dangerous situations. Their authority differs depending on the circumstances. In addition, an inadequate number of law enforcement officers (3,000) cover all of Indian Country. These officers patrol vast areas. For example, eleven of the twenty-five largest law enforcement agencies served jurisdictions covering over 1,000 square miles (Reaves 2011). TLOA attempts to resolve these issues with a number of approaches, including recruitment and retention strategies, creating and funding training protocols, and police access to federal databases.

Of special interest is that TLOA emphasizes the need to end violence against Indian women. It authorizes new guidelines for tribal authorities addressing sexual assault and domestic violence crimes. It also requires the Indian Health Service (IHS) to standardize sexual assault policies and protocols for handling evidence and interviewing witnesses of domestic and sexual violence crimes in Indian Country.

TLOA also requires training for all tribal judicial and law enforcement employees and BIA personnel about alcohol and substance abuse prevention for youth and adults. Training is also mandatory for narcotics investigations and prosecutions. Tribes would also benefit from incorporating cultural considerations into their codes, protocols, prevention, and training programs to ensure that they are integrated into law enforcement. This would in turn enhance tribal sovereignty.

Another important approach is cross-deputization. TLOA provides incentives through technical assistance and grants for tribal and state law enforcement agencies to enter into joint law enforcement agreements to combat crime in and near tribal lands. Importantly, TLOA expands the authority of tribal police to enforce federal laws regardless of the perpetrator's race. This makes it easier for tribes to exercise criminal jurisdiction thus providing more protection from crime in Indian Country.

With the passage of TLOA tribal courts may now prosecute felonies that federal authorities often considered not serious enough to pursue. TLOA amended the ICRA (1968) to allow prosecution of felony cases with sentencing of up to three years of imprisonment per crime and can be stacked up to nine years per case. Fines are limited to $15,000 per case (TLOA 2010). For tribal judiciaries to be eligible they must provide presiding judges who are licensed lawyers with sufficient legal training. In addition, defendants must be provided with an attorney licensed by the state or federal bar. Tribes are also required to be courts of record. Although this poses an additional burden on tribes, tribes may benefit from sharing information as they codify culturally appropriate rules and codes.

Relatedly, TLOA allows for federal prosecution of crimes not prosecuted by PL 280 states. Tribes may ask the U.S. attorney general to approve concurrent jurisdiction between the federal government, the state, and the tribe. Because the state's jurisdiction remains unchanged, PL 280 states no longer have to approve a change of status as previously required. This supports tribal sovereignty because it restores tribal jurisdiction over all misdemeanors and crimes perpetrated by Indians against Indians or non-Indians on tribal lands.

Tribes face serious obstacles for funding and developing critical infrastructure and programs. To address this, TLOA reauthorizes funding to support and improve tribal justice systems. Given that tribal incarceration capacity is usually only short term, a pilot program allows Indians sentenced for felonies in tribal court to be jailed in a federal facility at government expense. Alternatively, perpetrators may be imprisoned in tribal rehabilitation facilities, state facilities under contract with the tribe, or tribal facilities approved for long-term confinement by the Bureau of Indian Affairs (BIA). Tribally specific rehabilitation programs rooted in tribal traditions and values may be particularly helpful in promoting public safety and tribal sovereignty.

VIOLENCE AGAINST WOMEN ACT (VAWA)

In 1994, U.S. senator Joseph Biden sponsored the Violence Against Women Act as part of the Violent Crime Control and Law Enforcement Act (1994). Signed into law on September 13, 1994, it requires a coordinated community response to domestic violence, sexual assault, and stalking crimes, encouraging jurisdictions to engage multiple players to share experience and information to improve community-defined responses. VAWA 1994 also established grant programs through the Centers for Disease Control, the Department of Justice, and the Department of Health and Human Services. Specifically for Indian Country, VAWA 1994 included funding for a Department of Justice (DOJ) Services Training Officers Prosecutors Violence Against Indian Women (STOP VAIW) discretionary program. VAWA 1994 also created Tribes as States (TAS) status for creating and enforcing domestic violence and related codes. The program includes funds for training and technical assistance for tribal and state judges dealing with stalking and domestic violence cases. Of fundamental importance to Indian Country, the statute requires every tribe and state to give full faith and credit to protective orders issued by other tribes and states (Stevenson 1997, 8).

On October 28, 2000, President Bill Clinton signed the Violence Against Women Act of 2000 (VAWA 2000) into law under Division B of the Victims of Trafficking and Violence Protection Act of 2000. VAWA 2000 reauthorized essential programs, established new programs, and strengthened federal laws. Critical to tribes, VAWA 2000 funded grants to tribal coalitions, expanded interstate stalking laws to include cyberstalking, and added entering and leaving Indian Country to the interstate domestic violence and stalking crimes created by VAWA 1994.

The Violence Against Women Act of 2005 (VAWA 2005) was signed into law by President George W. Bush on January 5, 2006. This version authorized new programs and emphasized violence against Indian women, including culturally and linguistically specific services. The first DOJ Office on Violence Against Women (OVW) Tribal Consultation was convened at Prior Lake, Minnesota, with DOJ officials and tribal leaders. In 2007, the OVW made the first awards under the Grants for Tribal Governments program, which was more comprehensive than the original STOP VAIW program.

In 2008, the Section 904 Violence Against Women in Indian Country Task Force held its first meeting in Washington, D.C. On March 17, 2013, VAWA 2013 was reauthorized with Title IX, Safety for Indian Women, including Section 904 extending concurrent tribal criminal jurisdiction over violations of protection orders and domestic violence crimes involving non-Indians. Three tribes were chosen for pilot projects to expand their jurisdiction and implement Section 904 provisions: Pasqua Yaqui, Tulalip, and Confederated Tribes of the Umatilla Indian Reservation (DOJ 2014).

Support for Section 904 was strong, and numerous Native groups lobbied for the bill. Conservative lawmakers raised concerns that Section 904 might infringe on defendants' constitutional rights. As a result, the final version of Section 904 was written narrowly. It only covers violations of protective orders or domestic violence that occur on federally recognized tribal land. To be prosecuted, the perpetrator must live or work on the reservation, have an intimate relationship with a tribal member, or have a substantial tie to the tribe. In cases where the defendant might be imprisoned, Section 904 adds civil rights protections for tribal courts. It requires tribes to offer public defenders—at the tribe's expense—judges with legal training, a guarantee of effective assistance of counsel, and juries drawn from a cross section of the community.

Those civil rights provisions have already gotten a workout on three reservations, which have been prosecuting crimes as part of the Justice Department's pilot project since February 20, 2014. The experiences of pilot project tribes have exposed several jurisdictional gaps and the inability to bring charges for crimes that tend to occur alongside domestic violence, such as substance abuse, property destruction, threats, and stalking. It is problematic to prosecute domestic violence and leave other charges to federal or state authorities. As a result, tribal prosecutors may find themselves deciding whether to prosecute only some of the crimes or to let go of jurisdiction and refer cases to other agencies.

Under VAWA 2013, as of March 2015, all federally recognized tribes may exercise jurisdiction without permission from the DOJ. VAWA 2013 aims to recognize "the inherent powers of [a participating] tribe . . . to exercise special domestic violence criminal jurisdiction over all persons." However, another provision requires tribes to give defendants "all other rights whose protection is necessary under the Constitution of the United States" (VAWA 2013). This could be interpreted as requiring tribes to provide defendants with the constitutional rights they would have in federal or state courts, even though tribes are not subject to the Constitution.

LOOKING FORWARD

Even without a constitutional challenge, many tribes may not have the funding necessary to exercise VAWA jurisdiction. Tribes are eligible for federal funds, but they must compete for the grants, which takes a lot of work. Grants must be renewed regularly, require many administrative hours to manage, and can be used only for specific activities. VAWA 2013 called for up to $5 million in grants for tribes implementing Section 904, but as of the writing of this book, Congress has not appropriated the funds.

As a result, it has been difficult for tribes to develop and maintain the justice system infrastructure necessary for Section 904 jurisdiction. There is also concern that adopting Section 904 will undermine culturally specific court systems. The civil rights provisions of VAWA 2013 may even encourage some tribal justice systems to adopt a mainstream model. One way around that is that tribes could simply ask defendants to waive their civil rights to enter traditional courts, as state defendants sometimes do to enter drug diversion courts.

Jurisdictional complications are still a major hurdle for tribes. There remains a confusing tangle of tribal, federal, and state jurisdictional issues that depend on the location of the offense, the identity of the perpetrator, the identity of the victim, and the crime. TLOA does not resolve all these issues, but it does attempt to improve criminal justice in Indian Country.

As of 2017, of all the eligible tribes, nine were exercising TLOA's new sentencing authority, and eleven were close to implementation (National Congress of American Indians [NCAI] 2017). Ninety-six percent of tribes reported challenges due to funding limitations (GAO 2012, 3). Relatedly, two-thirds of the tribes who applied for funding in 2011 were ineligible because they did not have nonprofit 501(c)(3) status (GAO 2012, 4). It is also unclear how TLOA will affect criminal prosecution of non-Indians in Indian Country. On the bright side, declinations for federal prosecution went down to 34 percent by 2013 (DOJ 2013, 7). Although the act offers an opportunity to improve the justice systems in Indian Country, implementation will require improved communication and significant coordination among federal agencies and all components of tribal justice systems.

BENEFIT OF TRIBAL STALKING CODES

Tribes will do well to implement their own anti-stalking codes so that they can effectively address the problem of stalking. When writing codes, tribes will benefit from keeping a number of issues in mind. Definitions are of primary importance. For example, the difference between "implied threats" and "credible threats" can have a major impact on prosecution. Although an implied threat may seem benign to the casual observer, it may cause severe emotional trauma to a victim. A credible threat may require that an outsider would find the statement threatening. The more flexible the definition, the more room there is for the reality that in intimate violence situations context is everything.

Heightened care is necessary in code writing since ambiguous or overly specific terms may render codes ineffective. Some anti-stalking codes require intent to cause fear on the part of the stalker. In the case of the Eastern Band of Cherokee, their code requires that a person "willfully on more than one occasion follows, harasses or is in the presence of another person without legal purpose" (Cherokee Code 2001, Res. No. 20 (Supp. No. 2), Ch. 14–5.5(b)). The code states that harassment is "to engage in a course of conduct directed at a specific person that causes substantial emotional distress in such person and serves no legitimate purpose" (Cherokee Code 2001, Ch. 14–5.5 (a), (1)). This does not appear to require that a victim establish intent on the part of the perpetrator to cause emotional distress. It only requires a showing that the perpetrator intended to follow, harass, or be around the victim without a legal purpose. An example of a legal purpose is if the perpetrator picks up their children according to an agreed-upon schedule. The band's stalking provisions also address aggravated stalking. Aggravated stalking is when a stalker

1. makes a credible threat with the intent to place that person in reasonable fear of death or bodily injury; or
2. commits the offense when there is a court order in effect prohibiting similar behavior; or
3. commits the offense within five years of a prior conviction for this offense; or
4. the person stalked is a minor under 16 years of age (Cherokee Code 2001, Ch. 14–5.5 (c)).

The band's code defines credible threat as "a threat made with the intent to cause the person who is the target of the threat to reasonably fear for his or her safety. The threat must be against the life of, or a threat to cause bodily injury to, a person" (Cherokee Code 2001, Ch. 14–5.5 (a), (3)). It is important to keep in mind that requiring intent to cause fear is limiting because of the nature of stalking crimes. Many stalkers justify their actions because they think that their victims care for them and should know that there is not intent to inspire fear. Jettisoning the intent requirement for basic stalking crimes helps speed up prosecution and holds stalkers accountable for their actions regardless of their justifications.

Tribes will also benefit from considering culturally appropriate factors when drafting their stalking codes. One of the most important avenues for tribal self-determination is criminal justice because tribal communities can define themselves through codes and enforcement mechanisms (Washburn 2006). For example, the Law and Order Code of the Fort McDowell Yavapai Community allows for an expanded understanding of the family. This is important because familial structures in Indian Country are not usually limited to the nuclear family as they often are in the mainstream community. Their code considers stalking to include threats to a person and their immediate family (Law and Order Code of the Fort McDowell Yavapai Community, Arizona 1990, Sec. 6–58 (a)(1)). In this case, "'immediate family' means a spouse, parent, child or sibling or any other person who regularly resides in a person's household or resided in a person's household within the past six months" (Fort McDowell 1990, Sec. 6–5K (d)(2)). This allows for some inclusion of the value of extended family in traditional communities and recognizes the social impact of stalking on important social groups, not just the individual.

USING TRIBAL PROTOCOLS TO INCREASE SENSITIVITY TO STALKING CRIMES

Tribes may benefit from looking at examples of protocols from the mainstream community that has had more experience developing law enforcement protocols. However, tribes should use these as models only to create their own protocols tailored to their own communities and cultures. Protocols are useful administrative rules that take the guesswork out of executing established codes and policy. Effective protocols can prevent stalking crimes by helping officers to ask the right questions in order to establish a pattern of behavior that might otherwise be overlooked. Tribes would do well to develop formal criminal justice protocols to appropriately and effectively respond to stalking crimes. Some mainstream programs have dedicated teams of police officers, prosecutors, court personnel, and parole and probation officers from existing domestic violence units to deal with stalking (Hally 2002, 3). These teams have been trained to consistently investigate, monitor, arrest, and aggressively prosecute stalkers.

Although most tribes do not have the resources to create entire domestic violence or stalking teams, they may consider designating specific officers to handle domestic violence and stalking situations. Their expertise may become a resource for other tribal officers. In addition, they will have the opportunity to deal with victims every step of the way and throughout multiple incidents. If a victim is able to talk to a friendly officer who has experience and training in this field, she or he will be more likely to call for help.

CONSISTENT TRAINING EMPHASIZING CULTURAL VALUES

Consistent and regular training sessions on stalking and domestic violence policy and procedure are needed to ensure that all police officers are upholding department policies. This holds true in the mainstream community and should be doubly so in Indian Country due to low wages, high rates of police misconduct, and high attrition rates of tribal police officers (Barker 1998, viii–ix). Trainings must keep up with the turnover of law enforcement officers. To emphasize the importance of properly handling stalking and domestic violence situations, tribal chairpersons and council members should be involved in discussing these issues with officers. In addition, tribal elders should be brought in to discuss the control of intimate violence in tribal society and how it relates to traditional values and the roles of women and men in the tribe. It is very important that officers understand the vision of the laws regarding stalking and domestic violence. If they can see the whole picture of how violence affects the community, they may take those extra steps needed to prevent future harm. Tribal officers also need extra training in the use of federal interstate stalking laws as defined by VAWA.

CULTURALLY APPROPRIATE REMEDIES

Culturally appropriate remedies should function better than Western remedies in tribal communities. They take many forms, such as preventative ordinances and mediation procedures. The reemerging tactic of banishment may also be used for dealing with domestic violence and stalking situations.

A PREVENTATIVE ORDINANCE. An example of a way to integrate cultural concerns is the Hopi Preventative Ordinance. The policy section illustrates how traditional values do not condone family violence.

It is the policy of the Hopi Tribe to demonstrate *respect*, "kyap tsi" (Hopi) and "ag' ging" (Tewa), for members of the family and clan. The fundamental Hopi value of "kyap tsi" has long been practiced by the Hopi generations, and is reflected throughout Hopi tradition and culture. Abuse and violence against persons has a lasting and detrimental effect on (1) the individual who directly experiences the abuse, (2) the entire family and clan, who directly or indirectly experience the abuse, and (3) the Hopi Tribe, as the adverse effects of abuse and violence is perpetuated by succeeding generations and within Hopi society itself. The concept of "kyap tsi" and "ag' ging" incorporates a meaning of the family as sacred, or that which must be respected. The family as a fundamental unit of Hopi society, is an inculcator of traditional values. Accordingly, the family must exist in harmony. It is in the Hopi Tribe's best interest to bring the family, the clan and the Hopi Tribe together, to help one another towards a healthy future and for the common good. (Hopi Indian Tribe, Law and Order Code 1991)

This code does not deal with stalking specifically. The tribe uses the section on harassment to deal with stalking issues. Affirmative statements like this underlie the community's stance on family values. This may help prevent family violence and provide family members with firm footing when they seek to intervene in stalking and domestic violence situations.

MEDIATION

Navajo peacemaking stresses the importance of flexibility. Parties may seek redress through peacemaking either through court referral or self-referral. Peacemaking combines many avenues: "mediation, restorative justice, therapeutic intervention, family counseling, and Navajo teaching" (Coker 1999, 6). This flexibility allows space for creative remediation. Peacemaking is an example of how tribes may empower victims and the community when confronting their tribal criminal justice systems. However, there are potential problems with this. For example, the inherent issues with the balance of power in domestic violence situations may not be fully addressed if a victim feels pressured by the community to reach a settlement. If a perpetrator's family further victimizes the victim, the victim may want to back down and thus not receive the justice he or she deserves.

BANISHMENT CODES

Banishment or exclusion is another traditional approach that has been recently revived and appears to be supported by VAWA. Civil banishment codes are a way for tribes to control law and order within reservation boundaries without upsetting the precedent set in 1978 in *Oliphant v. Suquamish Indian Tribe* of federal jurisdiction over non-Indian offenders. Banishment codes usually emphasize a need for emergency exclusion of persons seen as an immediate threat to the life, health, or property of the tribe or any of its members. This method of social control could prove to be more effective than a tribal protection order when applied to some stalking situations.

The Eastern Band of Cherokee has a chapter in their code solely dedicated to the exclusion powers of the tribe that reads: "The Tribal

Council shall have the power to exclude enrolled Tribal members for sexual offenses against minors, and shall have the power to exclude other persons from Cherokee trust lands when necessary to protect the integrity and law and order on tribal lands and territory or the welfare of its members" (Cherokee Code 2001, Res No. 20 (Supp. No. 2), Part II, Chapter 2, Sec. 2–1). The definition of tribal territory is an issue since many reservations are checkerboarded and include non-Indian-owned fee lands. The Sault Ste. Marie Tribe of Chippewa Indians'Tribal Code specifies that "Tribal lands" include the "area over which the Tribe exercises criminal or civil regulatory jurisdiction, and includes . . . all lands within the exterior boundaries of the Tribe's reservation . . . and . . . all lands owned by the Tribe which are 'dependent Indian communities' under 18 U.S.C. 1151" (Sault Ste. Marie Tribe of Chippewa Indians Tribal Code 1995, Chapter 61: Barring Individuals From Tribal Lands, Sec. 102 Tribal Lands Defined, (1) and (3)). This could be highly effective for excluding perpetrators from reservation areas and provide victims of stalking with a greater sense of safety on the reservation.

Although some tribal codes are unclear, a number of them apply only to nonmembers and nonresidents, rendering them somewhat toothless. However, just as many of them apply to tribal members and legal residents. For example, the Sault Ste. Marie code authorizes the chairman "to order any person barred from Tribal lands for any reasonable cause related to the welfare of the Tribe, its property, members, business interest or the public interest" (Sault Ste. Marie 1995, Sec. 103, Chairman's Order, (I)) This includes members, nonmembers, residents, and relatives of residents of tribal lands. However, this code only allows banishment for up to one year.

Some exclusion codes address violations of banishment orders. A number of them make violation of the order a criminal offense. The Tribal Codes of the Hoopa Valley Tribe state that "any person who violates any order or part thereof issued pursuant to this Section shall be deemed guilty of an offense and, upon failure to comply with the order of the Court, may be sentenced to confinement for a period not to exceed six (6) months or to pay a fine of $500.00 or both, with costs, and ordered to comply with the previous order or amended order issued by the Court" (Hoopa Valley Tribe 1986). These banishment codes are just a few examples of the remedies readily available to tribes. Although most exclusion and banishment codes do not specifically mention crimes against women, tribes are using banishment against diverse perpetrators. Another possibility would be to use banishment followed by probation and behavioral modification training for perpetrators. This would help create a safe atmosphere on the reservation while demonstrating to the entire community that tribes are serious about law enforcement. These approaches could be useful for tribes seeking a means to address stalking and other criminal behavior against Indian women while expanding the assertion of tribal sovereignty.

EXERCISING TRIBAL SOVEREIGNTY TO END DOMESTIC VIOLENCE AND STALKING

One of the few areas where tribal sovereignty has been consistently upheld is with VAWA and TLOA. Divisions of the federal government have saved money and time by establishing government-to-government relationships with tribes so tribes can take over the administration of their own reservations. Tribes that do not establish these kinds of relationships with federal agencies will find it hard to maintain regulatory or legislative authority in the face of state challenges. Tribes must assert their jurisdiction wherever they can to prevent further destruction of their sovereignty.

The solutions to these problems are not simple. Tribes are faced with the awesome challenge of developing approaches to deal with constant change in the political and judicial climate. Tribes should take over as many of the aspects of reservation management as they can. The easiest way is to start with areas where they have been granted Tribes as States (TAS) status. This enables tribes to demonstrate that they are competent in numerous areas of policy and regulation development. Tribes should also focus on coalition building to rally support for new legislation supporting tribal sovereignty. One of the best ways for tribes to retain control over their reservations is to work within the framework of already approved forms of jurisdiction while not limiting themselves to those areas. This enables tribes to demonstrate their competence in numerous areas of policy and legal development, while also enhancing tribal sovereignty.

Tribes would do well to create codes that integrate local, cultural, and multidisciplinary responses to violence before they attempt to adopt and implement them. Tribes must develop formal criminal justice protocol to appropriately and effectively respond to violent crimes. They should form dedicated teams of police officers, prosecutors, court personnel, and parole and probation officers from existing domestic violence units. These teams should be trained to consistently investigate, monitor, arrest, and aggressively prosecute offenders. In addition, these teams need training in the use of federal interstate stalking and domestic violence laws as defined by VAWA. Tribes must also consider aggressively seeking multiple funding sources since they generally lack sufficient financial resources for enforcement. Although Section 904 is a step in the right direction, multiple barriers still prevent Native victims of violence in Indian Country from seeking the safety and justice they deserve.

Once tribes set about creatively using TLOA and VAWA, they may develop a multitude of tactics not only to address domestic violence on the reservation but to also further tribal sovereignty. The methods most likely to be successful are those rooted in tribal values and traditions. Coalition building and information sharing are also necessary. By designing, developing, and implementing their own culturally appropriate legal codes to address violent crimes against women, tribal governments will not only be able to protect their citizens, empower victims of violence, and hold perpetrators accountable, they will also further their sovereignty.

REFERENCES

Amnesty International. 2007. *Maze of Injustice: The Failure to Protect Indigenous Women From Sexual Violence in the USA*. New York: Author. https://www.amnestyusa.org/pdfs/mazeofinjustice.pdf.

Atwell, Mary Weick. 2002. *Equal Protection of the Law? Gender and Justice in the United States*. New York: Peter Lang.

Bachman, Ronet, Heather Zaykowski, Rachel Kallmyer, Margarita Poteyeva, and Christina Lanier. 2008. *Violence Against American Indian and Alaska Native Women and the Criminal Justice Response: What is Known*. Washington, D.C.: U.S. Department of Justice. https://www.ncjrs.gov/pdffiles1/nij/grants/223691.pdf.

Barker, Michael L. 1998. *Policing in Indian Country*. Albany, NY: Harrow and Heston.

Catalano, Shannan. 2012. *Stalking Victims in the United States—Revised*. Washington, D.C.: U.S. Department of Justice. http://www.bjs.gov/index.cfm?ty=pbdetail&iid=1211.

Coker, Donna. 1999. "Enhancing Autonomy for Battered Women: Lessons from Navajo Peacemaking." *UCLA Law Review* 47 (1): 1–111.

Deer, Sarah. 2003/2004. "Expanding the Network of Safety: Tribal Protection Orders for Survivors of Sexual Assault." *Tribal Law Journal* 4: 1–28. http://law school.unm.edu/tlj/tribal-law-journal/articles/volume_4/violence,%20women /index.php.

Department of Justice. 2013. "Indian Country Investigations and Prosecutions 2013." http://www.justice.gov/sites/default/files/tribal/legacy/2014/08/26/icip -rpt-cy2013.pdf.

———. 2014. "Justice Department Announces Three Tribes to Implement Special Domestic Violence Criminal Jurisdiction Under VAWA 2013." http://www .justice.gov/opa/pr/2014/February/14-ag-126.html.

Dunn, Jennifer L. 2002. *Courting Disaster: Intimate Stalking, Culture, and Criminal Justice*. Piscataway, NJ: Aldine Transaction.

Government Accounting Office. 2010. "U.S. Department of Justice Declinations of Indian Country Criminal Matters." GAO-11–167R. http://www.gao.gov /new.items/d11167r.pdf.

———. 2012. "Tribal Law and Order Act: None of the Surveyed Tribes Reported Exercising the New Sentencing Authority, and the Department of Justice Could Clarify Tribal Eligibility for Certain Grant Funds." GAO-12–658R. http://www.gao.gov/assets/600/591213.pdf.

Greenfeld, Lawrence, and Steven Smith. 1999. "American Indians and Crime." Washington, D.C.: U.S. Department of Justice, Office of Justice Programs. http://www.bjs.gov/content/pub/pdf/aic.pdf.

Hally, Jo. 2002. "Addressing Stalking in Native American Communities." *The Source* 2 (2): 1–4. https://victimsofcrime.org/docs/src/addressing-stalking-in -native-american-communities.pdf?sfvrsn=2.

Llewellyn, Karl N., and E. Adamson Hoebel. 1941. *The Cheyenne Way: Conflict and Case Law in Primitive Jurisprudence*. Norman: University of Oklahoma Press.

Murray, Virginia H. 1998. "A Comparative Survey of the Historic, Civil, Common, and American Indian Tribal Law Responses to Domestic Violence." *Oklahoma City University Law Review* 23: 433–57.

National Congress of American Indians. n.d. "Tribal Law and Order Resource Center." http://tloa.ncai.org/tribesexercisingtloa.cfm.

Reaves, Brian. 2011. "Tribal Law Enforcement, 2008." Washington, D.C.: U.S. Department of Justice, Office of Justice Programs. http://www.bjs.gov/content /pub/pdf/tleo8.pdf.

Stevenson, George B. 1997. "Federal Anti-Abuse Legislation: Toward Elimination of Disparate Justice for Women and Children." *Willamette Law Review* 33: 848.

Tjaden, Patricia, and Nancy Thoennes. 2000. "The Prevalence, Incidence, and Consequences of Violence Against Women: Findings from the National Violence Survey Against Women." Washington, D.C.: National Institute of Justice & the Centers for Disease Control & Prevention. https://www.ncjrs.gov/pdffiles1/nij/183781.pdf.

Washburn, Kevin K. 2006. "American Indians, Crime, and the Law." *Michigan Law Review* 104 (4): 709–77.

LEGAL RESOURCES

Assimilative Crimes Act 18 U.S.C.A. 13 (1825).

Cherokee Code, Res. No. 20 (Supp. No. 2), published by Order of the Tribal Council of the Eastern Band of Cherokee Indians, Chapter 14–5.5 (2001).

Duro v. Reina 495 U.S. 676 (1990).

General Crimes Act 18 U.S.C. 1152 (1817).

Hoopa Valley Tribe, Hoopa Valley Indian Reservation, Tribal Codes, Title 5: Exclusion Ordinance, Section IV: Violation of Order a Criminal Offense (1986).

Hopi Indian Tribe, Law and Order Code, Hopi Family Relations Ordinance, Subchapter 1, Section 2.01 (1991).

Indian Civil Rights Act 25 U.S.C. 1301 (1968).

Indian Self-Determination and Education Assistance Act 25 U.S.C.A. 450a–n (1975).

Law and Order Code of the Fort McDowell Yavapai Community, Arizona, Resolution No. 90–30 Chapter 6, Article III (1990).

Major Crimes Act 18 U.S.C.A. 1153 (1885).

Oliphant v. Suquamish Indian Tribe 435 U.S. 191 (1978).

Public Law 280 18 U.S.C.A. 1162 (1953).

Sault Ste. Marie Tribe of Chippewa Indians Tribal Code, Chapter 61: Barring Individuals from Tribal Land (1995).

Tribal Law and Order Act 25 U.S.C. 2801 (2010).

U.S. Bill of Rights (1791).

Violent Crime Control and Law Enforcement Act 42 U.S.C. 13701 (1994).

Violence Against Women Act 42 U.S.C. 13701 (1994, 2000, 2005, 2013).

7

ASSERTING SELF-GOVERNING AUTHORITY BEYOND THE FEDERAL RECOGNITION PARADIGM

North Carolina's Adaptation of the Indian Child Welfare Act

DANIELLE V. HIRALDO

ACROSS THE UNITED STATES, federally recognized tribes have been engaging in assertions of sovereignty and varying degrees of institution building associated with Native nation rebuilding. Jorgensen (2007) articulates the Native nation rebuilding principles as assertion of self-rule, capable governing institutions, culture match, strategic orientation, and public-spirited leadership. Much of the nation-building literature in the United States documents the successful strategies many federally recognized tribes use to build healthy and sustainable communities according to their own needs. These Indigenous self-government discussions often overlook state-recognized tribes.[1]

State recognition, much like federal recognition, serves as a tool for Native nations asserting varying levels of self-rule. In its broadest sense, state recognition establishes a government-to-government relationship with the state where Indigenous communities share geographical boundaries, unlike federal recognition that creates a direct political relationship with the federal government. Federal recognition standardizes how the federal government relates with Native nations using federal laws, policies, and regulations for guidance. In addition, the status recognizes important inherent rights for Indigenous peoples, such as the acknowledgment of

Indigenous boundaries and jurisdiction, ability to make and enforce a nation's own laws, ability to define citizenship requirements, and so on. Federally recognized tribes have the opportunity to engage in Indian gaming, access Indian-only programs, place land into trust, and many other opportunities. These advantages are why nonrecognized Indigenous peoples pursue the designation.

One fundamental difference between federal and state recognition is the government that recognizes the Indigenous nation's self-governing authority. Outsiders unaware of its functionality perceive the state recognition status as denoting authority and jurisdiction secondary to federally recognized Indigenous governments (Allen et al. 2007). State recognition does not replace federal recognition; however, the designation offers Native nations an alternative avenue to build a political relationship with an external government and create ways to assert self-governing authority. State recognition is not without disadvantages. The state designation constrains tribes as well. A standard for states to engage tribes does not exist as with federal recognition. From the state's perspective, state statutes, resolutions, and regulations govern the relationship. Koenig and Stein (2008) discuss how seventeen states that recognize tribes operate within seventeen different parameters. State rules and actions have the potential to constrain state-recognized Indigenous rights. However, these constraints have not prevented state-recognized tribes from engaging in nation-building activities.

One of the advantages overlooked when critically analyzing this designation is that state-recognized tribes are not bound to a hierarchical relationship with the federal government. It is in this flexibility where state-recognized tribes develop strategies to self-govern. Some strategies include negotiating a space within a specific political arena to assert self-governing authority. Hiraldo (2015) argues that as we begin to examine state-recognized tribes, we see Indigenous communities strategically engaging in governance outside of the federal government-to-government relationship. The fundamental question state-recognized tribal governments are tasked with answering is how to govern without the formal acknowledgment of specific rights. Furthermore, to what extent does working with states enhance or constrain nation building for state-recognized tribes?

Although Native nations and states have historically been at odds with one another, state-recognized tribes offer a different perspective on this relationship. A recent case of the tribal-state relationship from a state-recognized standpoint involves the state of North Carolina and Indigenous children. State-recognized tribes successfully influenced North Carolina officials to amend its juvenile code to insert a placement exception for state-recognized Indigenous children within the social services system. Inserting state-recognized tribes into the state's child placement process further expands on the notion that Indigenous peoples without the recognition of explicit rights can compel local and state governments to act in compliance with national interest. The national 1978 Indian Child Welfare Act (ICWA) excludes state-recognized tribes from child protections that federally recognized tribes enjoy. This exclusion requires state-recognized tribes to use other tools to protect their children from being placed outside of their community. This specific case demonstrates tribal-state collaborative efforts to provide for the welfare of state-recognized children neglected in the national legislation. In addition, this case exemplifies how federal political agendas can be implemented within state jurisdiction. This chapter briefly discusses ICWA and presents an overview of the strategies used by state-recognized tribes to negotiate their self-governing authority to provide for the welfare of their children.

This chapter assesses how state-recognized tribes in one state, North Carolina, are strategically developing government-to-government relations with state and local governments to assert specific Indigenous rights. This chapter neither focuses solely on the advantages and disadvantages of state recognition nor on the welfare of Indigenous children and the Indian Child Welfare Act. It seeks to demonstrate the efforts of state-recognized tribes to identify an issue—child welfare—and leverage their political relationship to negotiate a solution that recognizes self-governing authority and transcends the federal recognition paradigm. This example demonstrates how Indigenous communities can resist prescribed designations and solidify rights within a spatial context with tools at their disposal to achieve their own end.

TRIBAL-STATE RELATIONSHIPS

Common assumptions around tribal-state relations lead many scholars and practitioners to argue that states have no business in the tribal-national government-to-government relationship. Of the three foundational Supreme Court cases known as the Marshall trilogy (which include *Johnson v. M'Intosh* [1823] and *Cherokee Nation v. Georgia* [1831]), *Worcester v. Georgia* (1832) emphasized that states are not included in this exclusive relationship. Chief Justice John Marshall excluded states from interacting directly with Native nations and upholding national authority concerning Indigenous affairs. Further, the Marshall cases affirm a trust responsibility originating from negotiated treaties and extend to all federally acknowledged tribes. Pevar (2004, 32) explains that the court cases created an exclusive relationship "that obligates the government to keep its end of the bargain, now that the tribes have kept theirs."[2] Reality shows that the United States has not always, or even often, fulfilled fiduciary and other obligations of its trust relationship with Native nations.

During the early national period, states insisted that Indigenous communities sharing geographical boundaries be removed altogether. According to Rosen (2007, 15), "In their [states'] view, the presence of separate Indian communities within the state impeded white settlement, migration, use of natural resources, and implementation of transportation projects." Rosen recognizes that states were actively pursuing the removal of Native nations due to perceived hindrance of "progress." Moreover, states considered the federal government maintaining and asserting authority over Native nations within their boundaries a limitation of state sovereign authority. This tug-of-war for power created an atmosphere of contention between states and Native nations. In 1886, Justice Samuel Miller demarcated tribal-state relationships in *United States v. Kagama* (1886), arguing that

> They [Native nations] owe no allegiance to the states, and receive from them no protection. Because of the local ill feeling, the people of the states where they are found are often their deadliest enemies. From their very weakness and helplessness, so largely due to the course of dealing of the federal government with them, and the treaties in which it has been promised, there arises the duty of protection, and with it the power.

The "deadliest enemy" concept affirms Chief Justice Marshall's decision to exclude states from Indigenous affairs. This tension exists with good reason. States have actively undermined Indigenous peoples' rights, completely ignored tribal sovereign authority, and engaged in illegal land and resource takings (see also Fletcher 2007). For these reasons, states have garnered the reputation as the enemy.

To some extent the tribal-state relationship landscape has changed. The federal government has exercised plenary power in its legislation and policy to insert states into the exclusive relationship creating a wave of "new federalism" or "forced federalism." These new notions of federalism conceive states relating to Native nations in more ways than in the past. Forced federalism has occurred on a variety of occasions, as for example with the Indian Child Welfare Act (1978) and Public Law 83–280 (1953), where both pieces of legislation sought to transfer certain jurisdictions from the federal government to states.

The 1988 Indian Gaming Regulatory Act (IGRA) changed the way in which Native nations and states relate with one another. Immediately after the Supreme Court case *California v. Cabazon Band of Mission Indians* (1987) upheld tribal sovereignty and a tribe's right to establish gaming within its jurisdiction, congressional leaders passed IGRA. This act, among other things, required tribes pursuing Class III gaming to negotiate compacts with the state with which they share geographical boundaries.[3] Corntassel and Witmer (2008) argue the passage of IGRA initiated the "institutionalization" of tribal-state relationships, which requires each party to negotiate a compact agreement. Congress compelled tribes that entered the high-stakes gaming industry to negotiate gaming compacts with states. According to Corntassel and Witmer (2008, 5), "As a result of IGRA [Indian Gaming Regulatory Act] in 1988 and the subsequent transfer of federal powers to state governments, indigenous nations have now been *forced* into dangerous political and legal relationships with state governments that challenge their cultures and nationhood status" (emphasis in original). Federal legislation that requires tribal-state collaboration muddles the exclusive relationship parameters. Even though Supreme Court cases, the U.S. Constitution, and federal policies have affirmed that an exclusive relationship exists, Native nations, in an effort to assert their sovereignty, are interacting with states, counties, and other governments to address their own needs.

The changing political landscape has prompted Native nations to develop innovative strategies to exercise tribal sovereignty outside the exclusive government-to-government relationship. Steinman (2004, 96) declares, "Conversely, it [legal and political ambiguity regarding tribal status and rights] also has provided an opportunity for states and tribes to experiment and innovate politically, thereby exploiting one of the strengths of federalism." Even though an exclusive relationship exists, that does not suggest that federally recognized tribes are not relating with state and local governments. Cornell and Taylor (2000) describe this shift in government relations as a systemic devolution of power. According to Light (2008, 227), "As tribes and states negotiate the legal, political, and economic dynamics of Indian gaming, it is important to understand how tribal–state IGR [intergovernmental relationships] generate opportunities for and constraints on potential political partnerships." Gaming revenue provides opportunities for Native nations to actively influence state and local politics to engage in nation-building efforts outside of the exclusive federal relationship.

Federally recognized tribes creating strategies to circumvent the exclusive tribal-national government-to-government relationship is not new, especially concerning land and resource management. Wood and Welcker (2008) examine the use of private land holdings as a mechanism to conserve land and resources. Native nations are acquiring land through a conservation title or "fee title" in addition to the land into trust option, but some Native nations still acquire land in trust. Another mechanism Native nations use to protect resources is obtaining a conservation easement to protect the property. The fee title provides these nations with unrestricted ownership to the land, unlike the trust land status, on the other hand, they are subject to conservation mandates. More importantly, the conservation titles protect the land in perpetuity from development. Private land ownership risks severing trust ties but loosens the restrictions on land and resources that accompany trust land status. This shift in power is a departure from the exclusive relationship recognized in the U.S. Constitution, affirmed by federal legislation, and upheld by the Supreme Court. Native nations using these relationships as well as alternative strategies to engage in nation building demonstrate the possibility to leverage the political relationships with one government to compel another one to act in a Native nation's favor.

State recognition provides a different perspective on the Native nation–state relationship. *This relationship was not established as a means of inclusion but as a means of survival.* Understanding how and why this relationship has worked (or not) offers more examples of Indigenous communities interacting with state governments. More importantly, this perspective highlights strategies to facilitate the negotiation of competing interests through alternative arenas. Examining state-recognized/state relationships advances another perspective that demonstrates the potential for Indigenous people to leverage political authority over competing agendas found among national and state governments. It is important to note that the deadliest enemy concept implies that federal relationships are not highly contentious and contested. Both relationships are problematic. State-recognized strategies provide more alternatives for navigating state political relationships that any Indigenous nation could employ.

BACKGROUND: INDIAN CHILD WELFARE ACT (ICWA)

The passage of ICWA occurred during the 1970s when Indigenous leaders following the momentum with the Red Power movement began to aggressively insist upon self-determination and Indigenous rights. ICWA is a key piece of legislation that serves as a victory for those efforts. Prior to the passing of ICWA, public and private organizations placed Native children in non-Native homes at a high rate. ICWA sought to stop the across-the-board practices of removing Indigenous children. More importantly, the act acknowledges, according to Brown, Casey Family Programs, and the National Indian Child Welfare Association (2000), the cultural importance of Indigenous children being raised in Indigenous homes, as well as recognizing exclusive or concurrent (if within a PL 280 state) tribal jurisdiction over child custody proceedings including foster care placement, termination of parental rights, pre-adoption, and adoption placement. Many view this legislation as an affirmation of Indigenous rights to maintain self-governing authority when it comes to their children. ICWA legislation requires states to acknowledge and transfer jurisdiction from state courts to tribal courts if a child is taken into the state's child protective system. In addition, Fletcher, Singel, and Fort (2009) identify ways in which ICWA acknowledges exclusive jurisdiction over child custody proceedings within a Native nation. In its simplest terms, ICWA codifies the importance of familial connections within Native communities. A brief for *Adoptive Couple v. Baby Girl* (U.S. Supreme Court 2013) describes the act as recognizing "'the dynamics of Indian extended families,' which play a central role in Indian childrearing, and its determination that state courts had badly 'misunderstood' that dynamic." In addition to advocating for the transfer to tribal jurisdiction, ICWA supports Indigenous self-governance by acknowledging child well-being codes and laws adopted by Native nations as illustrated in Starks, Smith, Jäger, Jorgensen, and Cornell (2016).

Under federal Indian policy, however, state-recognized tribes are limited in their efforts to protect their children even though they are placed in non-Native homes just as frequently. Working from a disadvantage, Native nations operating outside of federal policy have to identify ways to protect their children and resist forms of injustice.

CASE STUDY: STATE RECOGNITION AND INDIAN CHILD WELFARE IN NORTH CAROLINA

North Carolina proclaims to share its territory with the largest Indigenous population east of the Mississippi River, with the majority belonging to state-recognized Native nations. There are eight state-recognized Native nations: Coharie Tribe, Eastern Band of Cherokee (federally recognized as well), Haliwa-Saponi Indian Tribe, Lumbee Tribe of North Carolina, Meherrin Indian Tribe, Occaneechi Band of Saponi Nation, Sappony, and Waccamaw-Siouan Tribe. The U.S. Census Bureau (2010a) identified approximately 9.5 million people living in North Carolina with 122,110 self-identifying as American Indian alone and 184,082 as American Indian in combination with another race. North Carolina's Commission of Indian Affairs (2010) gathered data from the same census and concluded that 73,345 people identified as one of the eight state-recognized Native nations in the state. Out of the one hundred counties in North Carolina, Robeson County maintains the largest Indigenous (Lumbee) population in the state, representing 38 percent of the county (U.S. Census Bureau 2010b).

Over the past ten years, the Indigenous communities in North Carolina have demanded more cooperation from the state to address the welfare of their children. In North Carolina, the Commission of Indian

N.C. TRIBAL AND URBAN COMMUNITIES

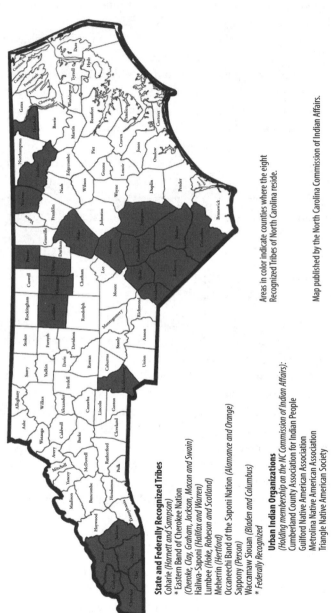

State and Federally Recognized Tribes
Coharie *(Harnett and Sampson)*
* Eastern Band of Cherokee Nation
(Cherokee, Clay, Graham, Jackson, Macon and Swain)
Haliwa-Saponi *(Halifax and Warren)*
Lumbee *(Hoke, Robeson and Scotland)*
Meherrin *(Hertford)*
Occaneechi Band of the Saponi Nation *(Alamance and Orange)*
Sappony *(Person)*
Waccamaw Siouan *(Bladen and Columbus)*
* *Federally Recognized*

Urban Indian Organizations
(Holding membership on the NC Commission of Indian Affairs);
Cumberland County Association for Indian People
Guilford Native American Association
Metrolina Native American Association
Triangle Native American Society

Areas in color indicate counties where the eight
Recognized Tribes of North Carolina reside.

Map published by the North Carolina Commission of Indian Affairs.

FIGURE 7.1 North Carolina Tribal and Urban Communities

TABLE 7.1 North Carolina 2001 Collaboration Statute Requirements

1) Establish a relationship between DSS and Indigenous communities in the state that will notify tribes once an Indigenous child is in the state's child protective system, and will consult on state placement policies

2) Agree on the process of identifying and recruiting NC Indigenous foster and adoptive parents

3) Agree on how NC child welfare workers and adoptive/foster parents will be educated and trained on Indigenous culture and history

4) Create an Indigenous child welfare advocacy team to partner with the Department of Health and Human Services

5) Develop a process to identify Indigenous children in the child welfare system

6) Identify the roles for both the state and tribal governments

Affairs (also referred to as the commission), a division of the Department of Administration, serves as an advocate for the Indigenous communities within the state. The commission received most of the child welfare–related calls in addition to an overwhelming number of inquiries and complaints concerning Indigenous child welfare practices for both state-recognized and federally recognized children. The lack of formal protocol to address these inquiries and the pressure to recognize the cultural distinctiveness of Indigenous children in North Carolina set the stage for legislative action.

In 2001, the North Carolina General Assembly enacted a statute that required collaboration between the state's Division of Social Services (NCDSS) and the Commission of Indian Affairs concerning Indian child welfare issues. The statute includes a clause that inserts state-recognized tribes into the collaboration efforts to "ensure successful means for securing the best interests of Indian children" (North Carolina General Assembly 2001).

The statute sought to communicate and address concerns of the Indigenous communities within the state. Not long after its passage, the commission created an Indian Child Welfare Task Force that has since become a standing committee. However, the state's Department of Social Services and local DSS agencies neglected to provide meaningful collaboration with the Indigenous communities as required by the statute. Many workers and practitioners were unaware that the statute was enacted.

Despite the requirement, several state tribes struggled to place their children within Indigenous homes. In 2007, the tribal government of Lumbee Tribe of North Carolina began to initiate local efforts to increase Indigenous foster parents with the assistance of the School of Social Work at the University of North Carolina (UNC) (Chamberlain 2009). Outside of the tribal government's partnership with UNC, individual tribal members began engaging North Carolina legislators to introduce legislation to protect state-recognized children and enforce the national Indian child welfare policy. The local newspaper reported on a discussion during a tribal council meeting: "Lumbee leaders want the Robeson County Department of Social Services to do more to ensure that Indian foster children are placed with Lumbee families. The Lumbee leaders say they are concerned the foster children may lose their cultural identity if they are placed in non-Indian homes" (Jenkins 2007).

Common factors among many state-recognized tribes are the importance of kinship and place. The community is made up of extended families, churches, and schools that have enabled them to maintain a strong sense of identity in a particular place. Oakley (2005, 12) describes identity: "Most Native Americans, including those in North Carolina, place tremendous importance on a sense of place—they came from here, whereas everyone else came from somewhere else. Therefore, their identity is intertwined with the local geography." The importance of place represents something literal, as Oakley explains with geography, but it also operates figuratively as an identifying marker of the community, including holding the same values and a common understanding of who they are as a people. Sustaining a connection to the children transfers and maintains Indigenous identity. The placing of children outside of the community jeopardizes the maintenance of that identity and in return jeopardizes the ability to sustain as a nation.

The pressure to address the placement of state-recognized children in state-recognized homes led North Carolina House representative Ronnie Sutton (Lumbee) to introduce a 2009 bill to the North Carolina General Assembly (2010) creating a House Study Committee to Preserve the Culture and Customs of Indian Children. The thirteen-member committee gathered information on "any issues or matters that would impact the preservation of the customs and culture of Indian children who are not covered under the Indian Child Welfare Act (ICWA) and who are the subject of legal proceedings in state courts, including adoption, custody, and visitation" (North Carolina General Assembly 2010). The report concluded:

> As of January 2010, there were 9,203 children in foster care. Of those, 118 were identified as American Indian/Alaskan Native. NCDSS does not have a mechanism to identify how many of the 118 children are federally recognized tribe members or state tribe members. There are currently 204 licensed Indian foster parents in the state. They are identified as American Indian/Alaskan Native. . . . While the ICWA only protects members of federally recognized tribes, children in the state recognized tribes are afforded similar consideration. North Carolina G.S. 143B-139.5A was enacted in 2001 to support collaboration between NCDSS, the NC Directors of Social Services Association and the Commission of Indian Affairs. The practical applications must occur in the County Departments of Social Services. (North Carolina General Assembly 2010)

North Carolina's state-recognized tribes argued that the need to identify a child's Native ancestry should not be limited to only federally recognized tribes. Even though the 2001 statute called for collaboration and subsequent bills were introduced to study the nature of state recognized children in the foster care system, no enforcement mechanism existed to ensure that collaboration occurred.

The momentum to adequately collaborate with state-recognized tribes and create significant relationships shifted after the state underwent a federally mandated Program Improvement Plan (PIP) in 2007. Each state undergoes a periodic Child and Family Service Review of its child welfare system. If the state is found to have areas of nonconformity set by national standards, it is required to develop a PIP. The PIP highlighted the state's inadequacies to properly identify Indigenous children (federal and state) early and consistently in the child welfare process.

To educate all parties involved on the Indigenous perspective of family and community, the National Child Welfare Resource Center on Legal and Judicial Issues and the National Child Welfare Resource Center for Tribes (NRC4Tribes) hosted a training/technical assistance conference in September 2011 that sponsored the eight tribes in the state, child welfare, and court partners. The North Carolina guardian ad litem associate counsel and co-chair of the Court Improvement Project (CIP) stated that the 2011 conference provided answers to many questions concerning issues involving Indigenous children from not only the perspective of federally recognized tribes but those from state-recognized tribes as well (Anonymous personal communication). After the conference, each of the parties sought to continue meaningful discussions to develop good practices for state tribe children in the child welfare system.

In Robeson County, the Lumbee Tribe continued to collaborate with the local department of social services to develop an intake form that identified Indigenous ancestry, either federal or state recognized, during the initial visit. The child protective service process typically begins with an incident report filed with DSS. Then, social workers conduct initial visits after an incident has been filed. If an incident is substantiated, proceedings begin to remove the child from the home and the state seeks appropriate placement. In the U.S. 2008–2012 American Community Survey five-year estimates, Lumbees represented approximately 40 percent of the children population in the county (U.S. Census Bureau 2012). Even with the large Lumbee population, a disparity exists between children in the foster care system and Lumbee foster care homes. In 2012, the Robeson County Department of Social Services noted sixty-four Native American children in the foster care system but only thirteen licensed Native American parents by the department (Gasque 2012). To build capacity, the tribal government worked with local churches to recruit more foster parents by holding informational sessions informing citizens of the requirements to become a foster parent.

The commission's Indian Child Welfare Committee strategically collaborated with North Carolina's Court Improvement Project (CIP) to assess North Carolina juvenile court performance. Established in 1995, CIP works with an interdisciplinary team that includes judges, attorneys, social workers, and others to review state statutes, improve courtroom practices and procedures, review cases from appellate courts, and so on. Typically, a bill proposed by CIP is reviewed and commented on by multiple parties before it is introduced to the General Assembly. Knowing CIP's success and well-established vetting process, Indigenous leaders approached it to develop a strategy to propose legislation that addressed state-recognized concerns.

The biggest implication of ICWA is that it upholds and recognizes exclusive tribal jurisdiction over child placement. North Carolina state tribes are within state jurisdiction and, as a result, federal jurisdiction.

Therefore, the state's attempt to collaborate with these communities could not contradict national legislation. Outside of the ICWA policy, all states are bound by general foster and adoption policy such as the 1994 Multiethnic Placement Act (MEPA) that declares children cannot be delayed or denied a home (foster care) based on their heritage, *except* race can be considered during the initial placement of children. MEPA provides specific exclusions for ICWA placement cases. CIP and the Indian Child Welfare Committee recognized that state legislation could not contradict national legislation, that is, MEPA, and had to negotiate with state tribes to guarantee that their children were considered.

With the assistance of the commission's Indian Child Welfare Committee, CIP identified a piece of legislation that could assist in coordinating with state tribes. In North Carolina, once a child is removed from the home, a hearing is held for placement called "placement while in nonsecure custody." Trying to expand state-recognized collaboration and keep within national regulations, the committee determined that ethnicity could be considered at the onset of placement as long as the child was not held from placement or taken away from a home because of race. North Carolina considers a hierarchy of options to determine child placement. The ideal placement once a child is removed from one parent is with the other parent. If the other parent is unavailable or both parents were together during the incident, then he or she is no longer considered. A relative is next in the priority hierarchy. If a relative is unavailable, a new definition, a "nonrelative kin," is required (Anonymous personal communication). The new definition seeks to comply with the exception in MEPA. It was introduced in House Bill 350: Court Improvement Project Juvenile Changes (a consensus bill), which proposed modifications to General Statute 7B-505 of the Juvenile Code. The changes to Section 13, "Placement while in Nonsecure Custody," inserted a new subsection:

> (c) If the court does not place the juvenile with a relative, the court may consider whether nonrelative kin is willing and able to provide proper care and supervision of the juvenile in a safe home. *Nonrelative kin is an individual having a substantial relationship with the juvenile. In the case of a juvenile member of a State-recognized tribe as set forth in G.S. 143B-407(a), nonrelative kin also includes any member of a State-recognized tribe or a member of a federally recognized tribe, whether or not there is a substantial relationship with the juvenile.* The court may order the Department to notify the juvenile's

State-recognized tribe of the need for nonsecure custody for the purpose of locating relatives or nonrelative kin for placement. The court may order placement of the juvenile with nonrelative kin if the court finds the placement is in the juvenile's best interests. (North Carolina General Assembly 2013)

Section 14, "Hearing to Determine Need for Continued Nonsecure Custody," includes a new subsection 2(a) with the same language as in Section 13 requiring the courts to consider "nonrelative kin" when placing members of state-recognized tribes. The new definition resembles ICWA provisions for placement hierarchy considering family members first, other tribal members second, and then other nonmember Native families. More importantly, it acknowledges the notion of place and space for state tribes. The new definition underscores that common values and cultural ties bind Indigenous peoples, which is important to consider when children are involved.

In June 2013, the governor signed the bill into law. The statute creates a way for state-recognized tribes to coordinate with local DSS agencies to address Native foster family recruitment efforts and child placement. The state has since formally adopted the intake form created in collaboration between Lumbee tribal officials and the Robeson County Department of Social Services. As Lana Dial, former Court Improvement Plan program director and Lumbee citizen, declared in 2013, "It's not a perfect answer, but it's a start."

The larger state-recognized community argued that the statute lacks teeth for enforcement and a lot of the authority remains with the courts to determine the "best interest of the child." The current statute also presumes adequate resources for state-recognized tribes to carry out these functions. Because communities are limited in their ability to assert tribal jurisdiction, this statute does not equate to the provisions within ICWA, but it does provide a distinctive example of political influence.

The statute continues an ongoing conversation with the state to address the needs of Indigenous communities. More importantly, it encourages the crafting of a more collaborative relationship with the North Carolina Department of Social Services through continuing education, webinars, and workshops, all dedicated to identifying Indigenous children in state-recognized communities and the importance of being a part of that

TABLE 7.2 North Carolina Provisions Compared to ICWA

NC ICWA	ICWA
Placement consideration hierarchy: 1) Parent 2) Family member 3) "Nonrelative" kin also includes any member of a state-recognized tribe or a member of a federally recognized tribe" (NC SL 2013–129)	Adoptive placement consideration: "A preference shall be given, in the absence of good cause to the contrary, to a placement with: (1) A member of the child's extended family; (2) Other members of the Indian child's tribe; or (3) Other Indian families." (25 U.S.C. 1915(a))

community. In 2015, a Memorandum of Agreement was signed between the North Carolina Commission of Indian Affairs and the North Carolina Department of Health and Human Services to continue collaboration and coordination for placement of Indigenous children within the state.

This example does not address the social ills that cause Indigenous parents to lose their children. What this case study does demonstrate is that state tribes can work within North Carolina's political system to address a critical issue that relates to who they are as a people. The national government played a role in this—it encouraged North Carolina to treat Indigenous child welfare issues appropriately—but its success did not depend on federal recognition.

NATION BUILDING BEYOND
FEDERAL RECOGNITION

The case demonstrates that state tribes serving as political actors have engaged tribal-state relationships to pursue specific agendas to meet the community's needs. At a big-picture level, the state tribes are building capacity by actively participating in the commission's Indian Child Welfare Committee and engaging politicians to find a remedy. These actions demonstrated the exercise of self-rule. The continued insertion into local, state, and federal politics highlights that state tribes are not waiting for one government or another to tell them they can or cannot govern. The ability to find a way to amend the preexisting North Carolina juvenile code to acknowledge state tribes concerning Native children welfare is a form of self-rule. State tribes identified an issue and found ways to insert their voice into the conversation even though specific rights were unconfirmed by the federal government. For the Lumbee Tribe, building capacity by holding informational sessions to recruit Lumbee foster parents and partnering with academic institutions were forms of nation building. In addition, the Lumbee tribal government worked with the local DSS to develop an intake form to track Indigenous children.

The active efforts of state tribes to assert their political influence at the state General Assembly to have their children considered, included coordinating efforts to provide for the welfare of the children neglected in the federal legislation (ICWA). Having an Indigenous representative in the state assembly provided a way to voice concerns that may have been overlooked otherwise.

This case highlights the complexity and flexibility of tribal-state relationships. It cannot be ignored that federally recognized tribes fought for the passage of ICWA. The problem, at least of *only* considering its constituency, is that the legislation neglects other Indigenous peoples in its definition. Using an established relationship and the commitment of North Carolina to state tribes, tribal leaders were able to work with local, state, and national agencies to pass the North Carolina legislation. Identifying a national policy, such as ICWA, compelled the state to act in compliance. North Carolina shares territory with eight separate Indigenous communities, and its willingness to listen to Indigenous concerns provided a ripe environment to leverage political influence to ensure the consideration of state tribes. One beneficial precursor of this collaboration is North Carolina's willingness to listen to Indigenous concerns to address needs in a culturally specific way. This is not a standard all states adhere to.

Being active participants in the political landscape has been key to the success of North Carolina state tribes. Their consistent ability to pursue a political agenda shows the political influence Indigenous peoples in the state have. Acknowledging that broad policy implication has an even greater political influence, tribal leaders identify arenas where the impact extends across communities and not just one. The legislation is not specific to one Indigenous community within the state but recognizes all children from North Carolina state tribes. The greater number of voices, the more likely someone is willing to hear and act.

Working with the state can also constrain nation-building efforts. Many of the state tribes rely on North Carolina law. An important aspect of nation building suggests nations create their own laws according to their own custom and traditions. This argument is not to suggest that all state tribes have neglected to craft their own laws. The North Carolina code states that the court may order DSS to notify the juvenile's state-recognized tribe for placement. Despite being under state jurisdiction, state tribal governments should actively craft and adopt their own child welfare codes reflecting how each government will approach responsibilities concerning their children in the state's child welfare system.

There are other ways to be proactive. State tribes can adapt strategies used by other Native nations across the United States, for example, the Fond du Lac Foster Care Licensing and Placement Agency. Fond du Lac was struggling with recruiting and licensing Native foster homes outside of its jurisdiction. The Harvard Project on American Indian Economic Development (1999, 247) found that "by establishing a separate non-profit entity, chartered under state laws, which then contracted the Fond du Lac government's Division of Human Services to provide all programmatic and administrative services, the band could legitimately work toward expanding the availability of Indian foster homes in northeastern Minnesota." The Houlton Band of Maliseet Indians located in Maine partnered and collaborated with the state on culturally relevant material for training and educating non-Maliseet providers (Harvard Project on American Indian Economic Development 2007).

State-recognized tribes can use such cases to further develop their collaboration efforts for child welfare issues. This adaptation strategy can be extended beyond child welfare issues and applied across other areas of concern by collaborating with state agencies or initiating policy revisions to effectuate change.

CONCLUSION

The child welfare example demonstrates how state-recognized tribes and states can collaborate on a government-to-government basis through a specific arena. The fact that this relationship is specific to North Carolina cannot be emphasized enough. North Carolina has a different history with relating to Indigenous peoples within its shared territory. In addition, the state has the largest Indigenous population east of the Mississippi River. Knowing these local political conditions is important in assessing whether a tribal-state relationship has the potential to work. An important takeaway from this case is that state tribes worked on one specific issue to find a solution with the state and building on its partnership can find ways to carve out other spaces to engage in nation-building efforts.

NOTES

1. I use *tribe* interchangeably with *Native nation* and *Indigenous*. For familiarity purposes, when I describe the different classifications (e.g., state-recognized) I chose to use *tribe* because of its common association.

2. Pevar (2004) suggests that negotiating treaties on behalf of the United States with Native nations was an economic strategy to avoid warfare and accumulate land. During the establishment years of the United States of America, most treaties with Native nations were treaties of peace and cessions of land.

3. IGRA defines Class III as "high stakes" games "commonly played at casinos, such as slot machines, blackjack, craps, and roulette" (United States. *An Act to Regulate Gaming on Indian Lands*. Washington, D.C.: U.S. GPO, 1988).

REFERENCES

Allen, Richard, Cara Cowan Watts, John Parris, Troy Wayne Poteete, Teri Rhoades, Tonia Williams, and Kathleen Wesho-Bauer. 2007. "Stealing Sovereignty: Identity Theft, the Creation of False Tribes." Paper presentation, Sovereignty Symposium XX, Oklahoma City, OK.

Brown, E. F., Casey Family Programs, and National Indian Child Welfare Association. 2000. *Tribal/State Title IV-E Intergovernmental Agreements: Facilitating Tribal Access to Federal Resources*. Seattle, WA: Casey Family Programs.

Chamberlain, Knight. 2009. "Sutton, Council Bump Heads." *The Robesonian*, April 17. http://infoweb.newsbank.com/resources/doc/nb/news/127BEAD ACD54EB08?p=WORLDNEWS.

Cornell, Stephen E., Jonathan B. Taylor, and Harvard Project on American Indian Economic Development. 2000. "Sovereignty, Devolution, and the Future of

Tribal-State Relations." Cambridge, MA: Harvard Project on American Indian Economic Development.

Corntassel, Jeff, and Richard C. Witmer. 2008. *Forced Federalism: Contemporary Challenges to Indigenous Nationhood*. Norman: University of Oklahoma Press.

Fletcher, Matthew L. M. 2007. "Retiring the 'Deadliest Enemies' Model of Tribal-State Relations." *Tulsa Law Review* 43 (1): 73–87.

Fletcher, Matthew L. M., Wenona T. Singel, and Kathryn E. Fort, eds. 2009. *Facing the Future: The Indian Child Welfare Act at 30*. East Lansing: Michigan State University Press.

Gasque, Conan. 2012. "Lumbee Leaders Seek Qualified Foster Parents." *SC Now*. http://www.scnow.com/news/state/article_3b490775-9bd3-5c5c-8776 -ba1367fb0233.html.

Harvard Project on American Indian Economic Development. 1999. "Fond du Lac Off-Reservation Indian Foster Care." Honoring Nations 1999. Cambridge, MA: Harvard University Press. https://hpaied.org/honoring-nations /nation-builders-in-action/honoring-nations-1999.

Harvard Project on American Indian Economic Development. 2007. "Indian Child Welfare Services." Honoring Nations 2006. Cambridge, MA: Harvard University Press. https://hpaied.org/sites/default/files/publications/Indian%20 Child%20Welfare%20Services.pdf.

Hiraldo, Danielle Vedette. 2015. *Indigenous Self-government Under State Recognition: Comparing Strategies in Two Cases*. PhD diss., University of Arizona.

Jenkins, Venita. 2007. "Lumbee Foster Families Scarce." *The Fayetteville Observer*, May 20. http://infoweb.newsbank.com/resources/doc/nb/news/119496FF65 AE455o?p=WORLDNEWS.

Jorgensen, Miriam, ed. 2007. *Rebuilding Native Nations: Strategies for Governance and Development*. Tucson: University of Arizona Press.

Koenig, Alexa, and Jonathan Stein. 2008. "Federalism and the State Recognition of Native American Tribes: A Survey of State-Recognized Tribes and State Recognition Processes Across the United States." *Santa Clara Law Review* 48 (1): 79–153.

Light, Steven Andrew. 2008. "Indian Gaming and Intergovernmental Relations: State-Level Constraints on Tribal Political Influence Over Policy Outcomes." *American Review of Public Administration* 38 (2): 225–43.

North Carolina Commission of Indian Affairs. 2010. "North Carolina American Indian Tribes by Population Group." Raleigh, NC: Author.

North Carolina General Assembly. 2001. "Collaboration between Division of Social Services and Commission of Indian Affairs on Indian Child Welfare Issues." General Statute 143B-139.5A. Raleigh, NC: Author.

North Carolina General Assembly. 2010. "House Study Committee to Preserve the Culture & Customs of Indian Children." Report to the 2010 General Assembly of North Carolina. Raleigh, NC: Author.

North Carolina General Assembly. 2013. "General Statute 7B-505 of the Juvenile Code." Raleigh, NC: Author.

Oakley, Christopher Arris. 2005. *Keeping the Circle: American Indian Identity in Eastern North Carolina, 1885–2004.* Lincoln: University of Nebraska Press.

Pevar, Stephen L. 2004. *The Rights of Indians and Tribes: The Authoritative ACLU Guide to Indian and Tribal Rights.* New York: New York University Press.

Rosen, Deborah A. 2007. *American Indians and State Law: Sovereignty, Race, and Citizenship, 1790–1880.* Lincoln: University of Nebraska Press.

Starks, Rachel Rose, Adrian T. Smith, Mary Beth Jäger, Miriam Jorgensen, and Stephen Cornell. 2016. "Tribal Child Welfare Codes as Sovereignty in Action." Conference edition. Paper presented at the National Indian Child Welfare Association Annual Meeting, St. Paul, MN, April 4–6.

Steinman, Erich. 2004. "American Federalism and Intergovernmental Innovation in State-Tribal Relations." *Publius* 34 (2): 95–114.

U.S. Census Bureau. 2010a. "North Carolina." Demographic Profile Data. American Fact Finder. http://factfinder.census.gov/faces/tableservices/jsf/pages/productview.xhtml?src=bkmk.

U.S. Census Bureau. 2010b. "Robeson County, North Carolina." Demographic Profile Data. American Fact Finder. http://factfinder.census.gov/faces/table services/jsf/pages/productview.xhtml?pid=DEC_10_SF1_SF1DP1&prodType =table.

U.S. Census Bureau. 2012. "Children Characteristics." 2008–2012 American Community Survey 5-Year Estimates. American Fact Finder. http://factfinder2.census .gov/faces/tableservices/jsf/pages/productview.xhtml?pid=ACS_12_5YR_S0901.

U.S. Supreme Court. 2013. "Brief for the United States as Amicus Curiae Supporting Affirmance." *Adoptive Couple v. Baby Girl, A Minor Child Under the Age of Fourteen Years, et al.* http://sct.narf.org/documents/adoptivecouplevbabygirl /us_amicus_brief.pdf.

Wood, Mary Christina, and Zachary Welcker. 2008. "Tribes as Trustees Again (Part I): The Emerging Tribal Role in the Conservation Trust Movement." *Harvard Environmental Law Review* 32 (2): 373–432.

LEGAL RESOURCES

Adoptive Couple v. Baby Girl 570 U.S. (2013).

California v. Cabazon Band of Mission Indians 480 U.S. 202 (1987).

Cherokee Nation v. Georgia 30 U.S. (5 Pet.) 1 (1831).

Indian Child Welfare Act § 1901 (1978).

Indian Gaming Regulatory Act 100–497 (1988).

Johnson v. M'Intosh 921 U.S. (8 W Wheat.) 543 (1823).

Multiethnic Placement Act 42 U.S. Code § 674—Payments to States (1994).

Public Law 83–280 codified in 18 U.S.C. § 1162, 28 U.S.C. § 1360 (1953).

United States v. Kagama 118 U.S. 375 (1886).

Worcester v. Georgia 31 U.S. (6 Pet.) 515, 8 L. Ed. 483 (1832).

U.S. Constitution (1789).

8

INDIGENOUS ON THE MARGINS

The Struggle to Address Juvenile Justice in the
United States and Aotearoa/New Zealand

EILEEN LUNA-FIREBAUGH AND
ANNE LUNA-GORDINIER

W HAT DOES IT MEAN to be sovereign in today's multilayered
and multicultural societies? Close looks at Indigenous communities reveal startling similarities in the Indigenous experience,
central among which is that Indigenous people live on the margins of
their societies. They are rarely an essential component of the dialogue but
rather often an afterthought. Indigenous populations may be viewed simply as representing a constellation of problems with which the colonizing
state must contend. They may be viewed as an example of the failure of
a modern state to contend with the challenges facing its citizens. But
for the Indigenous themselves, these failures of the colonizer states are a
continuing challenge to the progress necessary for the fulfillment of the
aspiration for sovereignty.

This chapter takes a close look at American Indians in the United
States and Māori in Aotearoa/New Zealand over the twentieth century
(Aotearoa is the Indigenous name of New Zealand). The emphasis is on
juvenile criminal justice and the attempts by these Indigenous communities to address the disproportionate punishment inflicted upon their
juveniles by the mainstream societies within which they live, and the new
attempts to accomplish diversion from juvenile misconduct. However, it is
inadvisable to consider only criminal justice. One must review the various
aspects of Indigenous life to have a complete picture of the challenges
faced by the Indigenous of these lands.

Both American Indians and Māori are Indigenous to their lands and struggle for the recognition of their Indigenous status by the nations within which they live. They struggle also for inclusion into the governments of their countries, for self-determination. They face significant detrimental criminal justice issues. They are largely urban, and most live under the authority of local or state governments. In the cities in which they live, police make very limited efforts to involve the Indigenous population in the operation of the law enforcement department, resulting in a low confidence level in law enforcement, regardless of attempts made by their respective police departments.

This chapter examines juvenile criminal justice for American Indians in the United States and Māori of New Zealand. It also examines relationships between colonizing entities and these communities, and the challenges they face in addressing disproportionate punishment inflicted on their juveniles by mainstream societies.

NATURE OF INDIGENOUS COMMUNITIES IN THE UNITED STATES AND AOTEAROA/NEW ZEALAND

There are 567 American Indian tribes in the United States, including 229 Alaska Native villages. As of the 2010 census, there are 2,932,248 American Indians, of whom 119,241 are Alaska Natives—approximately 1 percent of the American population (U.S. Bureau of Labor Statistics 2013). In comparison, there are approximately 1,300 marae in New Zealand (a marae is a meeting place registered as a reserve under the Te Ture Whenua Māori Act (1993) and the Māori Land Act/Te Puni Kōkiri (2009). According to the 2006 New Zealand census, 643,977 people had Māori ancestry, approximately 15 percent of the total population. According to the 2010 U.S. census, approximately 71 percent of American Indians are urban, as opposed to reservation-based. In New Zealand, more than 87 percent of Māori live on the North Island and in urban areas (Cormack 2007).

American Indian nations are sovereign. They have been deemed by U.S. courts to be "domestic dependent nations" with the right to make and enforce their own laws and to hold their police accountable to their own rules. American Indian nations also have authority in certain circumstances (for example, in contracting with local law enforcement) to define or restrict the assertion of state laws in Indian Country, a term defined in 1948 legislation by the U.S. Congress.

In contrast, pursuant to the Treaty of Waitangi signed by the British Crown and Māori in 1840, Māori are not considered sovereign (that is, having the right to make and enforce their own laws) and thus are subject to the laws of the state of New Zealand. However, recent legal cases have recognized limited self-determination and the Māori have begun to exercise the right to self-governance.

The experiences of both urban and reservation-based Indians and urban and rural Māori with the police are similar. Regardless of the location, American Indians and Māori, individually and collectively, often experience a disproportionate level of contact with police departments and local power structures as evidenced in statistics, stories, and reflections.

LEGAL STRUCTURES OF UNITED STATES INDIGENOUS SOVEREIGNTY

To understand the choices faced by American Indian nations and the decisions they make about juvenile justice, it is essential to understand tribal sovereignty and relevant laws. The relationship between American Indian nations and the colonizing nations began as that of independent sovereigns. Indian nations had the full independent authority to govern themselves. Treaty making with Indian nations from 1600 to 1871 included various land cessions, as well as other agreements with colonizing nations (Prucha 1994). Treaties are legally binding contracts between two sovereigns (Canby 1981). Indian treaties with the United States and the legal decisions that resulted protected the Indian nations' rights of self-government and self-determination and were protected by Supreme Court rulings as inherent to sovereigns, not something that had been granted to Indian nations by the U.S. Constitution.

Three U.S. Supreme Court cases in the early 1800s articulated the basis for the federal-tribal relationship: *Johnson v. M'Intosh* in 1823, *Cherokee Nation v. Georgia* in 1831, and *Worcester v. Georgia* in 1832, collectively known as the Marshall trilogy. Later, in *Morton v. Mancari* (1974), the Court firmly asserted that the sovereignty of American Indian tribes was inherent and predated the U.S. Constitution. With these cases, the U.S.

Supreme Court established that regarding American Indian tribal sovereignty, the federal government has plenary authority in Indian matters, not the states; Indian nations as sovereign domestic dependent nations have a legal trust relationship with the federal government and may not enter into agreements with foreign nations nor transfer their lands to any entity except the federal government; Indian treaties serve to uphold Indians' right of self-government; the courts should apply the rules known as the Canons of Construction in interpreting Indian treaties; and the protection of land guaranteed in treaties extends to the right to use and develop the resources of the land for the economic self-interest of Indian nations (Luna-Firebaugh 2007).

TREATIES AND THE CANONS OF CONSTRUCTION

In 1871, the United States ended the practice of treaty making with American Indian tribes; however, all treaties made prior to that year remain legally enforceable (Canby 1981). During the twentieth century, as cases arose that required the interpretation of preexisting treaties, the U.S. Supreme Court fashioned the Canons of Construction, a set of rules for interpreting treaties: first, treaties are to be interpreted as the Indians would have understood them at the time (*Tulee v. Washington* 1942); second, ambiguities should be interpreted to favor the Indian party or parties to the treaty (*Carpenter v. Shaw* 1930); and third, the whole treaty should be liberally interpreted in favor of the Indians (*Carpenter v. Shaw* 1930). In addition to rights of Indians specified in the treaty, any right not ceded in a treaty is reserved to the Indians (*United States v. Winans* 1905). These rules, along with the Marshall trilogy, set precedents for American Indian–federal government relations regarding juvenile justice.

AOTEAROA/NEW ZEALAND APPROACH TO THE SOVEREIGNTY OF THE MARAE AND THE RECOGNITION OF RANGATIRATANGA

As mentioned previously, unlike most American Indians, Māori do not have exclusive control over their lands but are deemed as having limited self-determination. A review of laws affecting their self-determination relative to juvenile justice follows. In the past, Māori were viewed by the British, similar to the British view of American Indians, as primitive savages; however, the very process of treaty negotiations establishes the recognition by the colonizer that the Indigenous people did possess enough sovereignty to sign a treaty, thus agreeing to the exchange of rights. The resultant treaty in Aotearoa/New Zealand has been viewed differently depending on the historical and legal eras. It has been considered in the following ways: as a document ceding absolute sovereignty with no recognition of residual Māori rights; as having no meaning in the colonizers' domestic law; as a sacred pact imbued with a unique constitutional spirit; and, in its most recent reincarnation, as a ceding of sovereignty balanced by limited Māori authority in areas circumscribed by the Crown (Hayward 1997).

The basis of Māori society is the marae, a ceremonial or sacred place that serves as the center of Māori society in a given area or with a given group. Legally a marae is a meeting place registered as a reserve under the Te Ture Whenua Māori Act of 1993. Legal interpretations have established that the marae are exempt from taxation and self-determined, that is, are controlled by Māori (Jackson 1995).

Since 1975, the Crown has redefined the Treaty of Waitangi, continuing to assert the cession of ultimate sovereignty by Māori but acknowledging a burden upon it, the need to acknowledge the right of *rangatiratanga* (Māori control of all things Māori). The British Crown now interprets the treaty to include some residual rights left to Māori by the treaty. These rights are not considered sovereignty but rather self-determination or self-management, subordinate to the right of the colonizer and the state (Jackson 1995). Although these rights focus mainly on land, they set precedent for relations between Māori and the New Zealand government.

MĀORI LANDS CASE, 1987

A 1987 land rights court case (*New Zealand Māori Council v. Attorney-General*) was the first to define treaty principles in some detail for New Zealand. The court's judgment became a precedent for later judgments and Waitangi Tribunal reports. The principles Judge Cook developed to render his decision echo the Canons of Construction in the United States, including the duty to act reasonably and in good faith by both parties to the treaty; that the duty of the Crown was extended to active protection of Māori people in the use of their lands and waters "to the fullest extent practicable"; that the government should make informed decisions relating to the treaty in order to act reasonably and in good faith; that the Crown should remedy past grievances—"If the Waitangi Tribunal finds merit in a claim and recommends redress"; and that the Crown has the right to govern. The principles of the treaty "do not authorise unreasonable restrictions on the right of a duly elected government to follow its chosen policy." Another judge in the case, Gordon Bisson, said it was "in accordance with the principles of the Treaty that the Crown should provide laws and make related decisions for the community as a whole having regard to the economic and other needs of the day."

Pursuant to these recently confirmed principles, the New Zealand Court has rendered a number of decisions that favor Māori rights ("New Zealand History" n.d.).

THE CHALLENGES WE FACE

American Indians and Māori, as citizens of a colonizing state, face many of the same challenges. These challenges are largely the result of systematic oppression and the lack of integration into society at large. In many ways the Indigenous remain defined as the "other," with reduced or little access to the systems that enhance opportunity. The Indigenous also suffer from the negative effect of disparate conditions, including poverty and unemployment, lack of health care, lack of access to the educational system, and the pervasiveness of the criminal justice system.

EDUCATION

Education is the key to societal advancement in many instances. Unfortunately for the Indigenous people of America and New Zealand, this advantage is not generally part of their experience. Almost 30 percent of American Indians (over the age of twenty-five) have not completed a high school education, as compared with 20 percent of the total population. One-third of American Indians living in tribal areas do not have a high school education, as compared with 20 percent of the total population. More than one half (55 percent) of American Indian youth fail to complete high school within six years. This compares negatively with the U.S. dropout rate for all students of 11 percent in 2000 (Bureau of Indian Education n.d.).

For Māori, the percentage of students leaving secondary education without qualifications was 36 percent, or almost double the national rate (Statistics New Zealand 2010).

EMPLOYMENT

The relationship between socioeconomic disadvantage and increased risk of later persistent offending has been well established, notwithstanding the effects of systemic bias and lack of opportunity. When one considers the Indigenous populations of the United States and New Zealand, this relationship is apparent. For example, American Indians are challenged by having one of the lowest employment rates in the United States. Only just over half (56.8 percent) of all American Indians over the age of sixteen are employed, as compared with more than 70 percent of the total U.S. population. The unemployment rates on many reservations exceed 60 percent to 70 percent (U.S. Bureau of Labor Statistics 2013).

The Māori unemployment rate (14.1 percent in 2013) is significantly higher than for non-Māori (6.8 percent) (New Zealand Ministry of Business, Innovation and Employment 2013). The juvenile unemployment rate for Māori was higher than for all others. Almost 18 percent of Māori males and almost 28 percent of Māori females ages fifteen to twenty-four were neither employed nor in school or training in 2012, as compared with a national average of 10 percent for males and 16 percent for females.

These problems faced by the Māori are seriously enhanced because their population is youthful—representing 36 percent of the total Māori population. Of these, 27 percent live below the poverty line (Statistics New Zealand 2010). Māori families have a 14 percent lower wage rate and during recessions lose jobs at a faster rate than Europeans.

CRIMINAL JUSTICE

In the United States, 43 percent of the American Indian population is under twenty years old, and in some tribes, the percentage is even higher. American Indian youth are arrested twice as often as other youth. Although they comprise 1 percent of the U.S. population ages ten to seventeen, nationally they comprise 2 percent of the arrests. One in twenty-five American Indians aged eighteen or older is under some form of criminal justice supervision, which is 2.4 times the per capita rate for white Americans and 9.3 times the rate for Asian Americans (U.S. Department of Justice 1999, 2006).

American Indian youth are 50 percent more likely than whites to receive the most punitive justice responses (for example, out-of-home placement after adjudication or waiver to the adult criminal justice system). In states where there are enough American Indians to allow for comparison, they are committed to adult prison at a much higher rate than that of white youth. The American Indian rate of incarceration in both prison and jails is 15 percent higher than the overall national rate. In 1997, 47 percent of American Indian offenders were confined in prisons or jails, as compared with 32 percent of non-Indians (U.S. Department of Justice 1999, 2006). The Tribal Issues Advisory Group is developing recommendations for federal sentencing guidelines in Indian Country for the United States Sentencing Commission. Their findings include that American Indian juveniles are overrepresented in federal jails and courts due to federal criminal jurisdiction on reservations.

Although there are no national statistics on juvenile recidivism, the U.S. Department of Justice (2006) presents average rates of recidivism for a select group of states. The study showed that juveniles released from incarceration were often rearrested within one year of their release. In general, juveniles released from incarceration have a one-year recidivism rate of 55 percent. In other words, 55 percent of juveniles are rearrested within one year of their release.

The Māori of New Zealand are also overrepresented at every stage of the criminal justice process. Though forming just 12.5 percent of the general population aged fifteen and over, 42 percent of all criminal apprehensions involve a person identifying as Māori, and 50 percent of all persons in prison are Māori (New Zealand Department of Corrections 2007). For Māori women, the picture is even more acute: they comprise around 60 percent of the female prison population. When one of the authors interviewed a senior police official who himself was Māori, he contended that more Māori were arrested because they committed more crimes, that this disproportionality was driven simply by statistics rather than by any form of bias against Māori (pers. comm., New Zealand Police Academy). This opinion flies in the face of research conducted by the authors and others that reveals the existence of disproportionality in detention and arrest.

Māori youth ages fourteen to sixteen amount to 23 percent of the total New Zealand population. Juveniles make up around 50 percent of all offenders, but in some youth courts the figure is as high as 80 percent or 90 percent. There were 22,589 police apprehensions for offenses by fourteen- to sixteen-year-olds, of which 54 percent were Māori (New Zealand Ministry of Justice 2001).

According to New Zealand police records, in 2012 approximately 28 percent of Māori juvenile apprehensions resulted in prosecution in youth court (Statistics New Zealand 2012). There are currently 4,000 Māori in prison, a number that is six times what one might otherwise expect. Further, another study of court criminal history data indicated that over 16,000 Māori males ages twenty to twenty-nine had served one or more prison sentences. This is approximately 30 percent of all Māori males in that age range, as compared with approximately 10 percent of non-Māori males. From 2000 to 2010 at least 3 percent of all Māori males ages twenty to twenty-nine were in prison, with non-Māori being less than one-sixth of this percentage. Owen and Te Puni Kōkiri (2001) revealed that Māori youth were three times more likely to be apprehended, prosecuted, and convicted than non-Māori youth. Recent Ministry of Justice statistics show that the apprehension rate for Māori youth aged fourteen to sixteen is more than twice as high as the rate for all young people and more than three times the rate for young people of other ethnicities. This disproportionality of Māori youth in the criminal justice system remains the subject of much discussion and evaluation.

Approximately 22 percent of Māori youth were dealt with by the Youth Aid Panel (the New Zealand specialist police section), 37 percent through "alternative action," and approximately 5 percent through "intention to charge Family Group Conferences" (some of which result in a charge being laid in the youth court) (New Zealand Ministry of Justice 2001).

MODELS OF INDIGENOUS JUVENILE DIVERSION

The similarities between American Indian and Māori youth are far-reaching. They include the forms that juvenile justice diversion programs take in different areas and the laws that guide them.

Juvenile diversion programs have been developed throughout the United States, including the Pima County, Arizona, system, the main example used in this chapter, where approximately 6,000 juvenile cases are supervised per year ("Pima County" 2010). In Pima County, an experimental juvenile justice program was enacted in 2002, with changes in 2008. These changes have reduced the American Indian juvenile detention population from more than 9 percent to 2.7 percent. This is a critical change because the simple fact of detention has repercussions. When an American Indian youth is detained in the criminal justice system, there is a 50 percent rate of recidivism attributable to the effect of detention itself (Long 2012).

Of these, 450 cases are handled in teen court and 500 are handled in juvenile court. From 2004 to 2008, American Indian youth were 34 percent more likely than non-Indians to receive a detention screening and thus to be considered for residential custody. From 2008 to 2010, this rate dropped to 14 percent. From 2004 to 2007, American Indian youth were one and a half times more likely to be placed in residential custody than white youth. From 2008 to 2010, this rate dropped to 49 percent, or less than half as likely as white youth. From 2008 to 2010, the percentage of American Indian youth referred to diversion, rather than to probation, more than doubled (from 4 percent to 8.5 percent). Those young people not referred to diversion remain on supervised probation. Pima County employs 127 probation officers who supervise the diversion program. The probation officers decide how and where an individual case is placed ("Pima County" 2010).

By mid-2012, thirty-five to forty cases were being referred to the Community Justice Board (CJB) program monthly. The CJB program is capable of handling ninety cases a month, but the county justice personnel do not use it to its fullest advantage. Chad Marchand, an American Indian and the director of the CJB program, contended that probation officers do not refer enough eligible cases that fit within their area of responsibility, which includes misdemeanors and Class 6 (lowest level) felonies.

The program has a number of elements, including a juvenile court center, community justice boards, and a high school diversion program. An emphasis is placed on education, which permeates every aspect of the program. This emphasis has been highly successful. For example, in 2009 more than 60 percent of the youth were not enrolled in school at point of contact. By the time their cases were closed, almost 75 percent of the juveniles were enrolled in an educational program (Long 2012).

An education consultant evaluation report was produced for April 2009 through March 2010 in which Pima County staff expressed their support of the system. The staff contended that the Disproportionate Minority Contact (DMC), Juvenile Detention Alternatives Initiative (JDAI), and Model Delinquency Court (MDC) initiatives developed in 2008 were responsible for raising the educational levels and for reducing recidivism by court-involved youth. They also asserted that the emphasis on early diversion, intensive interaction/mentoring, and focus on education created a restorative environment conducive to turning many lives around (Chandrasekharan and Feliz 2010).

PIMA COUNTY JUVENILE DETENTION CENTER

According to the Pima County Juvenile Court ("Pima County" 2010), more than 77 percent of the juveniles who went through diversion in 2010 did not reoffend. When the criminal history of graduates of the program was examined after they turned twenty-one, it was determined that more than 90 percent had no convictions as an adult. Further, more than 93 percent of juvenile probationers assigned to the Juvenile Intensive Probation Supervision (JIPS) program during calendar year 2010 were found to be drug-free. A close examination of JIPS revealed that positive change came about due to an emphasis on continued high school education.

The DMC/JDAI/MDC program mentioned earlier seeks to reduce both initial contacts and recidivism of youth. In 2007, the average daily detention population in the Pima County Juvenile Court Detention Center was 118. This number declined by 2012 to a daily population average of about fifty youth per day.

This dramatic reduction occurred even though the youth population of Pima County has increased. Juvenile delinquency criminal referrals also declined, from 11,500 in 2007 to 8,983 in 2010. Over these years, felonies decreased by 31 percent. In 2009, approximately 68 percent of all juvenile referrals were diverted from the formal court process. The Pima County Juvenile Court Detention Center has the only fully accredited high school in a juvenile hall in the United States. The program is focused on credit replacement to allow the juvenile to maintain his or her position in a traditional high school or to acquire a general education degree (GED) or special education where appropriate. The teachers are fully accredited and endorsed in the subjects they teach. When the academic liaison began her work within this program, there were three hundred young people on probation. As of 2012, there were only fifty youth participating in the Pima County diversion program. The academic liaison contends that this drop is a result of the number of youth who begin to complete high school and are successfully released from supervision (Long 2012).

COMMUNITY JUSTICE BOARDS (CJB)

Pima County Probation assigns selected cases to a network of twenty-one community justice boards staffed by 185 trained volunteers. Thirty-five to forty juvenile cases are received from Probation per month. The assignments are made for first- or second-time misdemeanors or Class 6 felonies. These include shoplifting/theft, alcohol consumption and/or possession, marijuana possession/paraphernalia, graffiti/damaged property, curfew violations, simple assault, and disorderly conduct (Chandrasekharan and Feliz 2010). The CJB program is a maximum of ninety days long depending on the decision made by members of the CJB and often includes conversations with the juvenile's probation officer and parents. The system is not based on the adversarial criminal justice system where wrongdoing must be proven by the prosecution; rather, youth are required to admit to the allegations in order to participate in the program. This admission is considered essential to full accountability and to the concept of restorative justice. The youth and parents sign a consequence agreement that sets out the expectations and establishes the consequences for failure to comply with the agreement and/or to complete the assignments. An essential element of the program is the writing of apology letters by the youth to their parents, the wronged party(s), and themselves. The letters flow from a belief that an apology is required to fully restore harmony and balance (Chandrasekharan and Feliz 2010).

The youth are also required to write essays assigned by CJB members. These essays differ depending on the CJB and needs of the juvenile. The concept flows from Tobias Wolff (1989), author of *This Boy's Life*. Community service is also a required component of CJB program completion and participation. This service is often tailored to the interests of the juvenile with the idea of advancing a focus on their future. Appropriate activities are then determined and the youth contacts the designated organizations. The CJB and the parents determine an appropriate length of community service assignments. The youth are also required to do home chores as determined by their parents in collaboration with the CJB. These chores include cleaning their rooms, cooking family meals, helping with younger siblings or pets, and other appropriate activities. Parents are requested to grade the youth on their performance on the assigned tasks. Students are also asked to reflect on their participation in these activities as well (participant observation, 2012).

The Community Justice Board program, with its focus on accountability and education, has been highly successful in reducing the recidivism rates among youth populations in Pima County. The program has an 82 percent compliance rate. The satisfaction rate for both parents and youth exceeds 95 percent of those surveyed. Whereas the national rate of reoffending within a year is more than 50 percent, the Pima County CJB has a recidivism rate of just 16 percent. The Drexel Heights CJB, located next to the Pascua Yaqui reservation, puts their recidivism rate at 12 percent. Not only do these rates compare very favorably with the national average, but they are also better than the traditional juvenile justice programs in Pima County. The traditional juvenile court has a recidivism rate of 30 percent and the teen court a rate of 16 percent (Chandrasekharan and Feliz 2010).

The Pima County CJB program is based on the concept of restorative justice and active civilian participants, where laypeople act on behalf of young people at disposition hearings pretrial. The aim of the program is to divert young people accused of crimes from detention while awaiting a court appearance. Those diverted receive appropriate community services, such as tutoring, drug counseling, and family counseling, along with intensive supervision. Their families also receive support, for instance, with child care or employment. Youth live at home or in an approved location.

Youth who opt to be included in the CJB must admit to the charge. They must sign a contract that they will participate in directed activities and return to or remain in school. They must remain in school until they are eighteen years old or have graduated from high school. Violation of this contract results in a determination of noncompliance and their case is returned to the court system. Upon satisfactory termination of the contract, their criminal record is expunged and there is no record kept of their charges.

The CJB is a panel of interested and trained volunteers, parents, and invited members of the youth's community. Police personnel and social workers do not participate. The victim of the youth's misconduct is not present but may provide a written statement about the action.

The effectiveness of this program has been evaluated by a number of studies including one conducted by one of the authors. Diverted American Indian youth had recidivism rates nearly 50 percent less than those detained in custody pretrial.

FUNCTION AND SUCCESS OF THE AOTEAROA/NEW ZEALAND FAMILY GROUP CONFERENCES

For Māori of New Zealand, disproportionality exists throughout the criminal justice system and extends to incarceration. The New Zealand youth justice system is based on the concepts of reintegration, restorative justice, diversion, and strengthening of the family. New Zealand has a well-developed formal child protective system. Its institutions include the family court, Child Youth and Family (CYF) Services (a government agency), foster parents "employed" by CYF, nongovernmental organizations (NGOs) that have contracts with CYF for the care of children, social workers with CYF and NGOs, and professional lawyers appointed by the family court to represent children. Lawyers appointed by the family court to represent children also work as general lawyers and receive special training to act as counsel.

International law is not incorporated into domestic law but must be taken into account when interpreting legislation and in the exercise of statutory discretion. The primary statute governing the legal representation of children in child protective proceedings is the Children, Young Persons, and Their Families Act of 1989 (CYPF). The CYPF Act provides "for the protection of children and young persons from harm, ill treatment, abuse, neglect, and deprivation." This legislation was enacted to make provisions for the extended family to be involved in making decisions concerning children and young persons in need of care and protection.

The following are essential elements of the CYPF Act. The purpose of this law is to promote the well-being of children, young persons, and their families and family groups. The law provides for establishing and promoting services and facilities within the community to advance the well-being of children, young people, and their families. These services and facilities are to be provided by those sensitive to cultural perspectives and aspirations of different racial groups, to be culturally appropriate for the values and beliefs of the juveniles and their families, and to be understood by and accessible to the juveniles and their families. Additionally, the law provides for assisting parents and families in preventing children from suffering abuse, neglect, or deprivation. Young offenders are required to be accountable for their actions but are also given opportunities to develop in responsible, beneficial, and socially acceptable ways in a system that acknowledges their needs.

GENERAL PRINCIPLES OF THE 1989 LAW

Five principles guide the application of the law: (1) the child's family, whanau (extended family), hapu (subtribe), iwi (tribes), and family group should participate in decisions that affect the child; (2) relationships among the child, whanau, hapu, iwi, and family group should be maintained and strengthened; (3) consideration must be given to the impact of decisions on the welfare of the child and whanau, hapu, iwi, and family group; (4) the wishes of the child must be taken into consideration; and (5) finally, the decisions affecting the child are to be made and implemented within a time frame appropriate to the young person's sense of time. Section six of the law makes it clear that the welfare of the child should be of paramount consideration in the application and implementation of the law to the child's situation.

The Family Group Conference (FGC) is an important element of the New Zealand youth justice system. In 2010 New Zealand passed and implemented a number of reforms to the juvenile justice system titled "The Fresh Start for Young Offenders Reforms." This legislation seeks to address recidivism by juvenile offenders and emphasizes the use of family group conferences. The FGC's youth are required to admit their acts of misconduct. Meetings include social workers, appropriate police officials, and members of the youth's family and community. Victims are also encouraged to participate, and approximately one-half do so.

A study titled "Evaluation of the Early Outcomes of Ngā Kooti Rangatahi" (New Zealand Ministry of Justice 2012) was established to reduce reoffending by Māori youth and to provide the best possible rehabilitative response by encouraging strong cultural links and meaningful involvement of the Māori community in the youth justice process. This process is a judicial-led initiative that locates part of the youth court process (monitoring of FGC plans) on a marae in an attempt to reconnect young offenders with their culture, improve their compliance with FGC plans, and reduce their risk of reoffending.

In this evaluation, judges and youth justice professionals identified two key challenges to the reduction of reoffending: first, the educational needs of Māori youth; and second, those youth engaged in education tended to be enrolled in alternative education programs. Although many had the potential to achieve in the mainstream education system, the options for transitioning Māori youth from alternative education back into mainstream education were very limited.

RANGATAHI COURT AND CONTINUING EDUCATION

Judges who participated in the aforementioned evaluation advised that a lack of options for placing disengaged Māori youth back into education or training was a common barrier. Unfortunately, the evaluation did not investigate the aspects of the wider youth justice system, such as FGCs. Nor did it seek to identify the medium- or long-term outcomes for Māori youth once they completed their FGC plan. The Ministry expressed its intent to undertake a quantitative analysis of recidivism of the young offenders who elect to participate in Ngā Kooti Rangatahi and an analysis of 282 discharges in the future.

Youth participants answered questions about their anticipated future educational endeavors and means to achieve their stated goals and were then questioned in depth about what activities they had engaged in to further their life plans. In one marae, a young man expressed an interest in military service. The judge discussed the linkage between New Zealand military service and Māori traditional values. The young man was encouraged to explore the professional opportunities in military and in police service and to report back to the rangatahi court during the next session. In this way the rangatahi courts were very similar to the Community Justice Boards of Pima County.

Interviews conducted by one of the authors with New Zealand police and Youth Aid officers found that young people responded best to close monitoring interactions that required the participation of the juvenile and systems of accountability. The development of accountable interactions with regional Youth Aid officers has resulted in a significant reduction in recidivism.

A meta-analysis conducted in New Zealand covering thirty-nine studies found that restorative justice approaches had more impact on reoffending by low-risk young people (8 percent decrease) than high-risk young people (1 percent increase) and some evidence that combining effective programs with restorative justice had 31 times more impact on reoffending by high-risk youth than restorative justice processes on their own (Latimer, Dowden, and Muise 2005).

The New Zealand juvenile diversion system based on the FGC research shows that programs effective for Māori youth generally take a holistic approach, involve relationships within the extended family or family type relationships, are tailored to the needs of individuals, and enhance cultural pride and knowledge of ancestry.

Although diversion and FGC procedures are an important step in the right direction, this system could be improved to enhance the inclusion of these factors in the youth justice system. Research suggests that improvements could be made to the system:

- In some circumstances insufficient efforts are made to include members of the wider Māori community.
- Māori offenders have criticized FGCs, saying they feel the process is focused on blaming them rather than on addressing the offending.
- Māori offenders often find interactions with police at FGC and in courts and prisons alienating and intimidating, or at least ineffective in addressing their problems.
- There is insufficient follow-up after FGC.
- Prisons and youth justice residences sometimes fail to address the causes of offending.
- There are few youth offending programs and services designed specifically by Māori for Māori. Effective programs should be staffed by Māori people with similar life experiences to their young charges.

The programs in New Zealand are relatively new, and there have been few comprehensive studies of the impact on reduction of juvenile recidivism. However, there is great hope vested in the transfer of juvenile cases to the marae. Reorientation of youth to the marae and to the traditional Māori leadership is viewed as a positive process, particularly given the willingness of Māori leaders to involve themselves in the juvenile rehabilitation system. In addition, it is widely believed that an emphasis on education of the youth—traditional, marae-based, and state-based—is resulting in a marked increase in recognition by the youth of future possibilities.

RECOGNITION OF THE INDIGENOUS NATURE OF THE PEOPLE

What does it mean to be Indigenous? Many Indigenous peoples in the United States and Aotearoa have defined it as an inherent connection to the land. The United Nations and international law define it as inhabiting a land before it was conquered by colonial societies and considering oneself as distinct from the societies currently governing those territories. However, the results of the authors' research seem to indicate that being Indigenous can mean a number of things, including a lack of involvement with the power structure; a failure of the government to address the myriad Indigenous needs, including education, land and property, and medical assistance; and a lack of Indigenous confidence in the police services provided by the government. Unfortunately, it apparently also means not being invited to participate in those issues that affect one's own life and the lives of those in one's community.

The effort to assert control over one's own life is essential if a people are to become fully participatory in the life of their nation. It is not enough to simply receive services, controlled and provided by others. This is paternalism.

Moves toward full sovereignty and self-determination are aided by laws and the commitment of political agencies. In the United States such laws are largely in place. However, only recently has the United States supported the UN Declaration on the Rights of Indigenous Peoples (2007). The expansion of rights enabled by international law has not yet occurred.

The assertion of sovereignty and self-determination by Indigenous communities has also proceeded on a de facto basis. For American Indians, the concept of de facto self-determination is that which results from the assertion of sovereignty, not the self-determination that arises from legal cases. American Indian tribes widely contend that if there is no law against something, the tribes have the right to undertake what they want to do, and they do not have to wait until this has been tested by the courts. For Māori, the assertion of land claims, the development of the rangatahi courts, and the integration into local and federal power structures are areas of potential success in the furtherance of Māori self-determination.

American Indians and Māori are also making efforts to insert themselves into the political arena and areas where they can provide services for their people. Often Indigenous people seek public funding to allow them to provide services for their own people, rather than seeking services from agencies to which public funding has been awarded. Further, it is important to recognize the extensive use of Māori language throughout New Zealand and the incorporation of Māori self-governance and educational concepts by the state. These have the potential to extend Māori self-determination in a way that differs from that of American Indians. It is through these efforts that the Indigenous of colonizer societies will be able to become fully responsible for their people.

REFERENCES

Bureau of Indian Education. n.d. U.S. Bureau of Indian Education website. http://www.bie.edu/Schools/index.htm.

Canby, William C., Jr. 1981. *American Indian Law in a Nutshell*. St. Paul, MN: West.

Chandrasekharan, Bhagyam, and Mark Feliz. 2010. "Annual Report: April 2009–March 2010. A Study of Best Practices for the Pima County Community Justice Boards, SWOT Analysis and Effectiveness Roadmap for CJB, December 2008." Pima County, AZ.

Cormack, Donna. 2007. The Māori Population. In *Hauora: Māori Standards of Health IV: A Study of the Years 2000–2005*, eds. B. Robson and R. Harris, 11–20. Wellington, New Zealand: Te Rōpū Rangahau Hauora a Eru Pōmare, University of Otago. http://www.uihi.org/wp-content/uploads/2013/02/Broadcast _Census-Number_FINAL1.pdf.

Hayward, Janine. 1997. "Appendix: The Principles of the Treaty of Waitangi." *Rangahaua Whanui National Overview Report* 2.

Jackson, Moana, 1995. *Māori, Pakeha and Politics: The Treaty of Waitangi, Sovereignty as Culture, Culture as Sovereignty: Māori Politics and the Treaty of Waitangi.* Sydney, AU: Global Cultural Diversity Conference Proceedings.

Latimer, Jeff, Craig Dowden, and Danielle Muise. 2005. "The Effectiveness of Restorative Justice Practices: A Meta-Analysis." *Prison Journal* 85 (2): 127–44.

Long, Rachael. 2012. Interview with Rachael Long, Pima County Youth Behavioral Specialist, April 3.

Luna-Firebaugh, Eileen. 2007. *Tribal Policing: Asserting Sovereignty, Seeking Justice.* Tucson: University of Arizona Press.

New Zealand Department of Corrections, Policy, Strategy and Research Group. 2007. "Over-representation of Māori in the Criminal Justice System: An Exploratory Report." http://www.corrections.govt.nz/__data/assets/pdf _file/0004/672574/Over-representation-of-Maori-in-the-criminal-justice -system.pdf.

"New Zealand History." n.d. New Zealand History. http://www.nzhistory.net.nz.

New Zealand Ministry of Business, Innovation and Employment. 2013. "Māori Labour Market Factsheet—March 2013." http://www.dol.govt.nz/publications /lmr/pdfs/lmr-fs/lmr-fs-Maori-mar13.pdf.

New Zealand Ministry of Justice. 2001. "Rangatahi Court. Evaluation of the Early Outcomes of Te Kooti Rangatahi." http://www.justice.govt.nz/publications /global-publications/r/rangatahi-court-evaluation-of-the-early-outcomes-of -te-kooti-rangatahi/publication.

New Zealand Ministry of Justice. 2012. "Evaluation of the Early Outcomes of Ngā Kooti Rangatahi." http://litmus.co.nz/wp-content/uploads/2015/11 /Evaluation-of-Nga-Kooti-Rangatahi-FINAL-report-17-December-1.pdf.

Owen, Victoria, and Te Puni Kōkiri. 2001. "Whanake Rangatahi: Programmes and Services to Address Māori Youth Offending." *Social Policy Journal of New Zealand* 16: 175–90. https://www.msd.govt.nz/documents/about-msd-and-our -work/publications-resources/journals-and-magazines/social-policy-journal /spj16/16-pages175-190.pdf.

"Pima County Juvenile Court Blueprint for the Future." 2010. http://www.pcjcc .pima.gov/Documents/Annual%20Report/Blueprint%202010.pdf.

Prucha, Francis Paul. 1994. *American Indian Treaties: The History of a Political Anomaly.* Berkeley: University of California Press.

Statistics New Zealand. 2010. "Secondary School Education." http://www.stats .govt.nz/browse_for_stats/education_and_training/secondary_education.

———. 2012. "Children and Young People Charged in Court—Most serious Offence Calendar Year." http://nzdotstat.stats.govt.nz/wbos/Index.aspx?Data SetCode=TABLECODE7361.

U.S. Bureau of Labor Statistics. 2013. "Labor Force Characteristics by Race and Ethnicity, 2012." http://www.bls.gov/cps/cpsrace2012.pdf.

U.S. Department of Justice. 1999. "American Indians and Crime." https://www .ojjdp.gov/ojstatbb/nr2006/downloads/NR2006.pdf.

U.S. Department of Justice. 2006. "Juvenile Offenders and Victims: 2006 National Report." https://www.ojjdp.gov/ojstatbb/nr2006/downloads/NR2006.pdf.

Wolff, Tobias. 1989. *This Boy's Life*. New York: Atlantic Monthly Press.

LEGAL RESOURCES

Carpenter v. Shaw 280 U.S. 363 (1930).

Cherokee Nation v. Georgia 30 U.S. 5 Pet. 1 (1831).

Children, Young Persons, and Their Families Act (1989).

The Fresh Start for Young Offenders Reforms (2010).

Johnson v. M'Intosh 21 U.S. 8 Wheat (1823).

Māori Land Act/Te Puni Kōkiri (2009).

Morton v. Mancari 417 U.S. 535 (1974).

New Zealand Māori Council v. Attorney-General 1 NZLR 641 (HC & CA) (1987).

Te Ture Whenua Māori Act (1993).

Treaty of Waitangi (1840).

Tulee v. Washington 315 U.S. 681 (1942).

United Nations Declaration on the Rights of Indigenous Peoples (2007).

United States v. Winans 198 U.S. 371 (1905).

Worcester v. Georgia 31 U.S. 5 Pet. 1 (1832).

CONCLUSION

KAREN JARRATT-SNIDER AND
MARIANNE O. NIELSEN

I NDIGENOUS PEOPLES in the United States, as noted in the beginning
of this volume, are often missing from the picture when examining
issues of criminal and social justice. Although federally recognized
tribal nations have, in some ways, become more visible in national policies
through legislation and presidential executive orders that acknowledge
the government to government relationship, they still represent a dimin-
utive percentage of the overall U.S. population, and so often have little
voice in the discussion of criminal and social justice. In contrast, as noted
in the introduction, they are the primary population discussed in other
colonized countries.

CONTINUING EFFECTS OF
COLONIZATION: CRIMINAL JUSTICE

Colonization is the underlying foundation for the chapters in this book,
for it set in motion loss of Indigenous lands, limitations on sovereignty,
ideas about Indigenous peoples that led to discrimination, and the framework for institutionalizing it all—first in colonial law and later in the laws
of the United States, Canada, Australia, and New Zealand. Falkowski
(1992, 1) traces the history of colonial law with the corresponding views of
Indigenous peoples as an inferior race and the institutionalization of it in
U.S. law, determining that "Indian law is race law." This notion is evident

throughout the history of federal Indian law and policy. For example, one of the early U.S. Supreme Court cases, *Johnson v. M'Intosh* (1823), relied in large part on the Doctrine of Discovery of the early 1500s to determine exactly what type of legal title American Indian tribes held to their own lands. This doctrine provided a framework for colonizing the New World based on religion. Those "discovered" peoples who were Christian were "civilized," whereas non-Christian peoples were heathens and "uncivilized." Because Christianity was an Old World religion, newly encountered Indigenous peoples were not Christian and thereby determined to be uncivilized. In *Johnson v. M'Intosh*, the Court justified its decision, saying that "although we do not mean to engage in the defence of those principles which Europeans have applied to Indian title, they may, we think, find some excuse, if not justification, in the character and habits of the peoples whose rights have been wrested from them." The Court decided that Indians held a title of occupancy, in perpetuity, but could not transfer their land to others.

Another example of Falkowski's characterization of Indian law is found in allotment policies of the late 1800s. Referred to by many as "allotment and assimilation" policy, the attempt to civilize the Indians and resolve "the Indian problem" was one of two primary objectives of allotment—the other being selling of "surplus" lands to non-Indians. Allotment was officially ushered in through the 1887 Dawes Act, turning reservation lands of certain tribes into individual parcels of land (or allotments). The purpose of breaking up reservations was to civilize the Indians (see Getches, Wilkinson, and Williams 1998, 141–50). Documents ensued from Indian commissioners and others on how to civilize Indian adults and especially children, from their perceived uncivilized, savage state to becoming civilized beings, possibly "fit" for becoming good citizens.

Colonization, then, is the thread pulled through time, predating the birth of the United States, Canada, and Australia but affecting the laws and policies pertaining to American Indians; Indigenous peoples of Australia, Canada, and New Zealand; and others. In the United States, from the inception of the country, policymakers sought to resolve what was designated "the Indian problem" and would continue to be defined as such until the more recent dawn of the era of American Indian self-determination in U.S. policy in the 1970s.

One of the many continuing impacts of colonization on Indigenous peoples is evident in the arena of criminal justice. Allotment policy of the 1880s has left some American Indian tribes with checkerboard lands, including parcels owned by non-Indians. In a 1978 case involving criminal jurisdiction within allotted Indian lands, U.S. Supreme Court chief justice Rehnquist reached all the way back to *Johnson v. M'Intosh* and selectively chose phrases from other, older Supreme Court opinions to support the majority's opinion in *Oliphant v. Suquamish* (1978) that American Indian tribal nations did not have criminal jurisdiction because it was "inconsistent with their status."

Another federal Indian policy era, the termination and relocation era (1950s–1960s), has left a lasting impact on criminal justice in Indian Country that remains a significant factor making criminal jurisdiction on Indian lands a highly complex puzzle. Public Law 280 (1953) mandated state criminal jurisdiction in Indian Country in a handful of states and made it optional for other states—regardless of the wishes of affected American Indian tribes. Further complicating this issue is that Public Law 280 was later rescinded in some states fully and partially in others. Social justice issues are often related to Indigenous criminal justice issues.

Additionally, as the authors in this book have shown, for Indigenous peoples and their communities, sovereignty—the right to make decisions for themselves—affects the lives of their citizens every day, in critical ways, from the right to administer effective justice grounded in cultural values to economic development within the borders of their own territory. In turn, it affects social justice issues such as discrimination toward Indigenous athletes, the basic human right of Indian women to bear children, and freedom from fear of becoming victims of hate crimes.

American Indian sovereignty in U.S. federal law is elastic, a result of U.S. Supreme Court and other court decisions and interpretations of sovereignty as well as legislation. That is, at times sovereignty has been defined narrowly—often by U.S. Supreme Court decisions—constraining the authority of federally recognized Indian nations, in some instances over criminal jurisdiction within their own borders. The term *sovereignty* is used pervasively both in Native communities and in discussions about them. In the United States, the legal definition derives from the Marshall trilogy of U.S. Supreme Court cases, where tribes were deemed *domestic dependent nations*, with the right of self-government subject to limitations by the federal government (Getches et al. 1998, 72–147). As noted, through the various twists and turns of decades of federal Indian policy, Indian sovereignty saw more limitations imposed, particularly in the arena of criminal justice. However, since the era of American Indian self-determination in U.S. federal policy, the interpretation of sovereignty has often been broadened or reinforced through legislation, as Archambeault points out.

The American Indian self-determination policy era has seen numerous pieces of legislation and presidential executive orders. Many support the broader understanding of tribal sovereignty and refer to the government-to-government relationship between federally recognized American Indian tribes and the United States (see, for example, Executive Order 13007 [1996] concerning sacred sites or Executive Order 13157 [2000] concerning tribal consultation). Luna-Gordiner's discussion of tribal authority under the Tribal Law and Order Act (2010) and the Violence Against Women Act offers other examples of how more recent federal legislation enhances tribal authority within their own borders, increasing their ability to better protect women from violence. In some cases, American Indian nations' sovereignty was narrowed even as it was upheld by the U.S. Supreme Court, as in *Oliphant*, and in some cases it was reinforced, as Bennett points out in her discussion of Indian gaming and the *Cabazon* case. However, Class III Indian gaming also led to the decision in *Seminole Tribe of Florida v. Florida* (1996). In that decision, the Court struck down a provision within the Indian Gaming Regulatory Act (1988), which allowed tribes to sue states after 180 days if the state refused to negotiate a Class III gaming compact in good faith. The topic of Indian gaming itself shows the elastic nature of American Indian tribal sovereignty, offering examples where sovereignty has been strengthened by the courts and at least one example of where it has been narrowed.

CONTINUING EFFECTS OF COLONIZATION: SOCIAL JUSTICE

As noted earlier, colonial legal practices and views of Indigenous peoples became institutionalized in laws of various colonizing nations, notably, but not only, in the United States, Canada, Australia, and New Zealand. Indigenous peoples continue to suffer effects of colonization leading to a host of social justice issues. Robyn notes that because of their status as members of an ethnic group considered inferior or undesirable, large numbers of American Indian women were sterilized without their consent, not only robbing them of their ability to bear children but also leaving many with emotional and possibly irreparable harm. It is noteworthy that, regardless of the arguable applicability of the United Nations' Convention on the Prevention and Punishment of the Crime of Genocide (1948) to U.S. citizens at the hands of their own government or agents thereof, the practice of involuntary sterilization of American Indian women would be considered a violation of Article 2 (d) of that act: "imposing measures intended to prevent births within the group." At the very least, it remains a striking, everlasting example of the continuing impact of colonization suffered by Indigenous peoples and discrimination against them.

That same discrimination extends to border towns, as Bennett discusses, where it sometimes erupts into hate crimes against Indigenous individuals, where the criminal justice system sometimes fails to find justice for the victims. Ali-Joseph sheds light on another area of discrimination resulting in social injustice. Stereotypes about American Indian athletes in some cases leads to discrimination against them in college sports and, in turn, creates barriers to education for those student athletes. Such discrimination can serve to obstruct an avenue to higher education and subsequent economic and career opportunities for those students.

CRIME AND SOCIAL JUSTICE IN INDIGENOUS COMMUNITIES: LOOKING TOWARD THE FUTURE

The topics within crime and social justice discussed by the authors in this volume raise questions such as these: Where does this leave Indigenous peoples in the twenty-first century? What does the future hold for the rights of Indigenous nations and Indigenous peoples to regain control over their lives—their citizens, their resources—and to be able to administer justice within their own borders and communities?

Both American Indian nations and Indigenous peoples in the United States and other countries are taking action to claim authority and put strategies into play, regardless of legal decisions or legislation. Notably, the legislation the authors discuss applies to federally recognized American

Indian nations, ignoring the numerous Indigenous nations within the United States who still lack federal recognition, as Hiraldo points out. Hiraldo explores how a state-recognized Indian tribe has been successful in working with the state government to exert authority over child adoption and foster care, in effect exercising "on the ground" sovereignty where they lack such status under federal law. Beyond U.S. borders, Luna-Firebaugh and Luna-Gordinier describe how the Children, Young Persons, and Their Families Act (1989) of New Zealand provides opportunities for the Māori to provide effective, culturally appropriate juvenile justice services for youth and their families.

Building relationships with states and local governments can be successful, particularly for non–federally recognized tribal nations. Fostering government-to-government relationships with state and local governments will be increasingly important, especially in areas where non-Indian population growth brings Indigenous and non-Indigenous communities into proximity, with implications for environmental, criminal justice, and social justice issues among neighboring communities.[1] Furthermore, Indigenous nations can look for opportunities to assume authority to implement federal legislation on their lands. Those opportunities represent critical junctures in Indigenous nations' increasing ability to more fully realize self-determination. In cases where authority is devolved (that is, assumed by tribal, state, or local governments), the assumption of that authority by tribal nations is an act of sovereignty. However, if Indigenous nations don't act to assert their authority then states may assume it, claiming jurisdiction to implement the law in Indigenous communities. This may erode Indigenous sovereignty, depending on American Indian–state relations in a particular state.

On one hand, American Indian nations in the United States have seen strides forward in reinstating their inherent sovereignty, through legislation supporting self-determination in general and expanding (or returning) tribal jurisdiction within Indian Country in particular cases. In other areas, legislation has responded to the potential impact on and interest of American Indian nations, for example, in land management practices of forests managed by federal agencies, such as the Tribal Forest Protection Act (TFPA) (2005). The TFPA gives federally recognized tribal nations the opportunity to conduct stewardship projects on those adjacent federal lands for the purpose of preventing wildfires (or other threats) that start on federal lands from running over Indian lands. The TFPA is but one of several recent examples, in addition to those already mentioned, of legislation enhancing American Indian sovereignty.

Astutely, though, Native nations are not simply waiting for the law to return authority to them. Indigenous nations and communities are practicing sovereignty and concretely moving forward to make decisions for themselves, employing de facto self-determination. De facto self-determination, as used here, differs significantly from the usage of the term *self-determination* in international law, particularly the United Nations Declaration on the Rights of Indigenous Peoples (2007). De facto self-determination is the practice of Indigenous nations and communities asserting authority by developing programs and services that address some of the many social justice areas described in this book and others.

De facto sovereignty practices also may prove to be an effective way for Indigenous peoples to withstand any future court decisions that narrow, or snap back, the legal interpretation of sovereignty and may address intertwined social justice issues. More and more Indigenous communities are engaging in programs to address diabetes and other health issues by asserting food sovereignty, for example. Food sovereignty as discussed here uses the definition delineated at the international Forum for Food Sovereignty (2007) as "the right of peoples to healthy and culturally appropriate food produced through ecologically sound and sustainable methods, and their right to define their own food and agriculture systems." Tohono O'odham Community Action (n.d.) is an example of an organization that revives traditional agriculture and sustainable foods and in doing so is trying to address health issues, such as diabetes, through traditional foods, which are low in sugar and provide protein and complex carbohydrates—all factors in reducing diabetes risk.

De facto sovereignty also includes Indigenous nations creating new legal codes to address criminal justice issues that affect Indian women, youth, and all citizens to address safety, health, and well-being—basic everyday needs—all of which have been dismantled to one degree or another by colonization, many of which still affect Indigenous peoples today.

Today when Indigenous peoples are discussed, more and more scholars approach the specific issues addressed through the lens of resilience. Rather than the former approach of examining issues as deficits within

Indigenous communities, a resilience approach asks what factors have contributed to the success of Indigenous communities despite the challenges of succeeding. Although used in various academic disciplines from public health to American Indian and Indigenous studies, no single definition of resilience exists. However, all definitions include "the capacity to face challenges and to become somehow more capable despite adverse experiences" (LaFromboise, Hoyt, Oliver, and Whitbeck 2006, 194). De facto sovereignty—the responses of Indigenous communities themselves to the challenges they face, despite legal obstacles and many other challenges—can be understood through the lens of resilience. Despite all obstacles, Indigenous individuals and communities are finding ways to assert their sovereignty de facto and are finding positive solutions to issues that have continued to confront them for many years. Some of the chapters within this volume offer examples of such Indigenous resilience.

As more Indigenous nations continue to actively assert their sovereignty—governing their own citizens in effective ways that reflect their foundational cultural values and meet their needs—their communities benefit. They will continue to move toward thriving nations and communities, and perhaps colonizing nation-states will continue to make progress in supporting self-determination for Indigenous peoples. Future research should examine more aspects of de facto sovereignty as well as state-tribal relationships in the United States. Perhaps one day scholars will be able to refer to the harmful effects of colonization as a long and shameful chapter of the distant past. As Indigenous nations and communities create and offer more programs and services that affect the lives of their peoples in a positive manner—from forging child welfare agreements with states, to taking charge of their youth in criminal justice systems, to creating their own legal codes—Indigenous peoples are putting the "self" into self-determination in very real ways that matter for their peoples. As these innovative and culturally sound programs find success, they contribute to healthy, resilient Indigenous communities where Indigenous peoples turn to their own nations and leaders to find justice.

NOTE

1.   The Gila River Indian community borders local communities in the Phoenix metropolitan area as does land of other American Indian nations. A

quick look at any land status map of Arizona will show American Indian lands bordering metropolitan Phoenix area cities.

REFERENCES

Falkowski, James E. 1992. *Indian Law/Race Law: A Five Hundred Year History*. New York: Praeger.

Forum for Food Sovereignty. 2007. *Declaration of the Nyéléni*. Sélengué, Mali. http://www.tocaonline.org/food-sovereignty.html.

Getches, David H., Charles F. Wilkinson, and Robert A. Williams Jr. 1998. *Federal Indian Law: Cases and Materials*, 4th ed. St. Paul, MN: West.

LaFromboise, Teresa D., Dan R. Hoyt, Lisa Oliver, and Les B. Whitbeck. 2006. "Family, Community, and School Influences on Resilience among American Indian Adolescents in the Upper Midwest." *Journal of Community Psychology* 34 (2): 193–209.

Tohono O'odham Community Action. n.d. www.tocaonline.org.

LEGAL RESOURCES

California v. Cabazon Band of Mission Indians 480 U.S. 202 (1987).

Children, Young Persons, and Their Families Act (1989).

Convention on the Prevention and Punishment of the Crime of Genocide (1948). https://archive.org/details/un1948genocidearticle2definition.

Dawes Act. Statues at Large 24, 388–91 (1887).

Declaration on the Rights of Indigenous Peoples (2007). http://www.un.org/esa /socdev/unpfii/documents/DRIPS_en.pdf

Executive Order of the President 13007, signed May 24, 1996. "Indian Sacred Sites."

Executive Order of the President 13175, signed November 6, 2000. "Consultation and Coordination with Indian Tribal Governments."

Indian Gaming Regulatory Act PL 100–497 (1988).

Johnson v M'Intosh 21 US (8 Wheat) 543, 5 L.Ed. 681 (1823).

Oliphant v. Suquamish Indian Tribe 435 U.S. 191 (1978).

Public Law 280 18 U.S.C.A. 1162 (1953).

Seminole Tribe of Florida v. Florida 517 U.S. 44 (1996).

Tribal Forest Protection Act 25 U.S.C. §3115a (2005).

Tribal Law and Order Act 25 U.S.C. 2801 (2010).

Violence Against Women Act 42 U.S.C. 13701 (2013).

CONTRIBUTORS

Alisse Ali-Joseph (Oklahoma Choctaw) earned her PhD from the University of Arizona. Dr. Ali-Joseph joined the Applied Indigenous Studies family at Northern Arizona University in 2013 and specializes in the importance of sports and physical activity as a vehicle for empowerment, cultural identity, health, and educational attainment for American Indian individuals. She also focuses on American Indian health and wellness and American Indian education. Dr. Ali-Joseph was appointed by the president of Northern Arizona University as the faculty athletics representative in fall 2015. In this role, Dr. Ali-Joseph works with the athletic department to maintain academic integrity with student athletes and faculty and ensure the overall well-being of student athletes.

William G. Archambeault (French, Ojibwa, and Lakota ancestry) earned his PhD in criminology from Florida State University. He taught for over a quarter of a century at Louisiana State University in Baton Rouge, where he was professor and chair, Department of Criminal Justice, and professor of social work. After retirement, he served as professor and chair, Department of Criminal Justice, at Minot State University in Minot, North Dakota, and adjunct professor in the Doctoral Program in Criminal Justice at the University of North Dakota in Grand Forks. For more than two decades, his academic scholarship focused on American Indian and Alaska Native crime and justice issues, publishing or presenting more than a dozen papers or book chapters on Indian justice topics. For many years, he was an Ojibwa sun dancer and sweat lodge leader, working with medicine leaders of different tribes and incorporating this learning into his academic work. He is presently retired in Rockport, Texas, where he keeps actively informed on and involved in American Indian issues.

Cheryl Redhorse Bennett (Diné and Comanche) is an assistant professor at Arizona State University and from Shiprock, New Mexico. She has a doctorate from the University of Arizona in American Indian studies and earned a master of arts degree in American Indian studies from the University of California, Los Angeles. Her research interests explore social issues in Indian Country including race relations, crime, and hate crimes against American Indians, with a focus on reservation border towns. Bennett previously held positions working in American Indian and tribal education and was a visiting professor at Fort Lewis College in Durango, Colorado.

Danielle V. Hiraldo (Lumbee) serves as the outreach specialist/senior researcher at the Native Nations Institute (NNI), a department within the Udall Center for Studies in Public Policy (UC) at the University of Arizona. In 2015, she received a PhD from the American Indian Studies program at the University of Arizona in Tucson. She holds an MPA and a BA in political science with a concentration in prelaw from the University of North Carolina at Pembroke. Danielle's research examines how state-recognized tribes are asserting self-governing authority outside of federal acknowledgment. More broadly speaking, her research analyzes tribal-state relationships and Indigenous governance. Prior to continuing her education, Danielle worked for her own tribe assisting with federal recognition efforts, among other responsibilities.

Lomayumtewa K. Ishii (Hopi) is an artist from the village of Sichomovi, First Mesa, on the Hopi Reservation in northern Arizona. He is of the Rabbit/Tobacco clan and is a Hopi practitioner of religious activities and Hopi dry-farming agriculture. He has recently completed an artist fellowship at the School of Advanced Research in Santa Fe, New Mexico.

Karen Jarratt-Snider (Choctaw descent) is an associate professor and chair of the Department of Applied Indigenous Studies at Northern Arizona University. Her expertise is in the areas of Indigenous environmental justice, federal Indian policy, tribal administration, and tribal environmental management. She has over fifteen years of experience working with tribal nations' projects in applied community-based research. Her work engages three critical areas for Indigenous peoples: environmental management and policy, policy and administration, and sustainable economic development—all of which coalesce around the overall topic of Indigenous sovereignty and self-determination. She teaches Indigenous environmental justice and federal Indian policy and law, and was a curriculum designer and lead instructor of the Tribal Environmental Management course for the Institute for Tribal Environmental Professionals at Northern Arizona University.

Eileen Luna-Firebaugh (Choctaw and Cherokee) is retired from the American Indian Studies program at the University of Arizona. She is an attorney and a member of the California Bar. She also holds an MPA from the Kennedy School of Government at Harvard University, where she was awarded both the Christian Johnson Endeavor Foundation Native American Fellowship and the John B. Pickett Fellowship in Criminal Justice. She is an appellate judge for the Colorado River Indian Tribes, with jurisdiction in both Arizona and California. She is a faculty member of the National Tribal Judge College, funded by the U.S. Department of Justice. She was principal investigator for the National Institute of Justice evaluation of STOP Violence Against Indian Women programs, and for a National Institute of Health study of family violence programs in Australian Aboriginal communities. She was also a consultant to the Harvard CIRCLE Project, a joint U.S. DOJ and tribal project on juvenile justice. She is the author of *Tribal Policing: Asserting Sovereignty, Seeking Justice* (University of Arizona Press, 2007) and a number of articles on tribal policing and tribal administration.

Anne Luna-Gordinier (Choctaw and Cherokee) is an assistant professor at California State University, Sacramento. She earned a PhD in sociology from Howard University in 2014 and a law degree and MA in

American Indian studies from the University of Arizona in 2004. She teaches on social theory, social inequality, gender, environmental justice, and social movements. Her research in Native American sociology focuses on radical criminology, environmental justice, urban Indians, and women's leadership.

Marianne O. Nielsen is a professor in the Department of Criminology and Criminal Justice at Northern Arizona University. Her expertise is in justice issues affecting world Indigenous populations. She teaches an undergraduate-level course, Native Americans and Criminal Justice, and a graduate-level seminar, World Indigenous Peoples and Justice. She has worked for Native organizations and has done research in Indigenous communities. She is co-editor with Robert Silverman of *Aboriginal Peoples and Canadian Criminal Justice* (Toronto: Harcourt Brace, 1992), *Native Americans, Crime and Criminal Justice* (Boulder: Westview, 1996), and *Criminal Justice in Native America* (University of Arizona Press, 2009); and with James W. Zion of *Navajo Peacemaking: Living Traditional Justice* (University of Arizona Press, 2005). She is also the co-author with Barbara Heather of four articles about Quakers and American Indians.

Linda M. Robyn (Anishinabe descent) received her doctorate from Western Michigan University in 1998. She is a professor in the Department of Criminology and Criminal Justice at Northern Arizona University in Flagstaff. Her current research interests include American Indians and the criminal justice system, sterilization of American Indian women, environmental justice including uranium and coal mining resource acquisition, and the effects of state-corporate crime on American Indian nations.

INDEX